SUCCESS
HABITS

*Eleven Steps to Becoming an
Uncommon Achiever!*

Greg Powe

Success Habits
by Pastor Greg Powe

Published by Revealing Truth Ministries
5201 N. Armenia Ave.
Tampa, FL 33603

Unless otherwise noted, all Scripture quotations are from the King James Version of the Holy Bible.

Cover design by M&N Design Company

Library of Congress Cataloging-in-Publication Data:
International Standard Book Number:
0-09702097-0-3 01 02 03 04   0-09702097-0-3
Printed in the United States of America

Dedication

I would like to dedicate this book to my wife, Deborah, and our children: Greg, Christopher, Bryan and Chrystle.

Contents

Introduction

Making Success A Habit

My mind is a habitat for success. It is a place where successful thoughts can be found and formed.

Not all habits are bad. As a matter of fact, success is a lifestyle that is paved by certain decisions and choices that have become so commonplace that you no longer think about doing them. In other words, they become success habits.

Success is defined as "a favorable outcome." The word *habit* means "a manner of conducting oneself, or a behavior pattern acquired by frequent repetition." Therefore, we can define success habits by asking ourselves the question: *What can I do repetitively that will produce a favorable and desired outcome in my life?*

Success Habits is an instruction manual on how to build a successful life-style by learning and developing habits. Throughout these pages, I've answered this question by drawing from the chapters of my own life experiences and from the powerful wisdom of the Bible. Since I've paved the pathway of my own life with these success habits, I know that they will work for you, too.

All true success starts with God. The Bible is filled with records of men of God who made a habit of being successful. They were men who displayed success habits.

One was Joseph, who was consistent in his commitment to what God told him to do. Genesis 39:3 says, "When his master saw that the Lord was with him and that the Lord gave him success in everything he did…" (NIV).

No matter what Joseph's circumstances were, nothing changed his vision. The way that Joseph thought about his vision from God became a success habit, and God brought success to everything he did.

The Bible says this about David: "In everything he did he had great success, because the Lord was with him" (1 Sam. 18:14, NIV). David made a habit of being successful because he had no fear. In the face of great opposition, David remained faithful to what God had said about him. He made it a habit to be the person God said he was, and he never caved into what the devil or other people tried to recreate him to be.

Uzziah was another successful man who made success a habit. In 2 Chronicles 26:5, we read: "He sought God during the days of Zechariah, who instructed him in the fear of God. As long as he sought the Lord, God gave him success" (NIV).

Uzziah made a habit of seeking God before he did anything, seeking Him consistently and constantly. When God gives us a vision, many of us may seek Him intensely about that vision for a season. But when that vision begins to come to pass, or when we lose interest or it becomes more difficult than we expected, we stop seeking God. However, Uzziah's success habit of seeking God and not quitting, even when times were good, brought him great success throughout his lifetime.

Success has a habit of creating a large following. In 1 Chronicles 12:23-38, we see how David's success caused mighty men to follow him. Just a few of the long list of names of important, powerful and notable people who followed David are listed below from this passage:

These are the numbers of the men armed for battle who came to David at Hebron to turn Saul's kingdom over to him, as the Lord had said:

> *Men of Judah, carrying shield and spear—*
> *6,800 armed for battle; Men of Simeon,*
> *warriors ready for battle—7,100; Men of*
> *Levi—4,600, including Jehoiada, leader of the*
> *family of Aaron, with 3,700 men, and Zadok,*
> *a brave young warrior, with 22 officers from*
> *his family;...*

All these were fighting men who volunteered to serve in the ranks. They came

> *to Hebron fully determined to make David king*
> *over all Israel.*
> —1 Chronicles 12:23-26,38, NIV

Developing your own success habits will put you in the company of great and successful leaders, and it will cause many others to follow you. Habits of success will release the greatness that God placed within you and allow you to walk in a new way with confidence and strength.

The Bible says this about mankind, *"as he thinketh in his heart, so is he"* (Prov. 23:7). The way you think about yourself, your life, your God and your future will determine who you are and how successful you will become.

Principles to Build Habits

Success is a result of applying certain biblical principles of wisdom over and over again in your life. Through repetition, you will find that you begin to enact these principles subconsciously. A habit is nothing more than something you do over and over until it becomes second nature to you. When that occurs you will begin to realize that you have changed—your thinking has changed. You have developed habits of success based upon biblical principles, and you will begin to discover that success results from everything you do.

Chapter by chapter, as you read through this book, you will discover eleven powerful habits that can become a part of your life. These habits are created and built upon the principles listed below. Therefore, I'd like to outline these principles in order to provide you with a foundation for the success habits that you'll be learning throughout this book. Let's take a look:

Principles of Success

Principle No. 1
Become a dreamer

Solomon was a dreamer who decided to do something that had never been done before. That's what dreamers do. Dreamers also provide jobs and increase for those around them who refuse to dream, and they stretch the imagination of everyone in their paths.

If you are a dreamer, you probably challenge everyone around you, for dreamers thrust average people into the zone of greatness.

Being a dreamer doesn't always come easy. In building your dream, you will experience rejection and jealousy and become the brunt of other people's opinions. They may call you money hungry, materialistic and greedy.

Principle No. 2
Develop a passion for your dream

Solomon knew what he wanted and he had plenty of passion for his dream. Dreamers are born, not borrowed. Your dream must be birthed inside of you and it must be your own, God-given dream.

In order to develop a dream, ask yourself what you would attempt to do if you knew it was impossible to fail.

Principle No. 3
Make wisdom the obsession and goal of your life

Solomon sought for wisdom, which was the most important thing possible.

Principle No. 4
Cultivate godly self-confidence in your ability to achieve your dreams

Solomon cultivated godly self-confidence that he could achieve his dreams. Godly self-confidence creates an atmosphere that affects your thoughts and creates a miracle climate. Solomon grew up with greatness as David's son. But he never killed a bear or lion, never went to battle or killed a giant. What Solomon had was the "weapon of humility."

Principle No. 5
Know your personal limitations

Nobody knows everything. Solomon recognized that he needed a power greater than his own (see 1 Kings 3:7). Everyone of us has weaknesses. Some know our limitations, but few acknowledge them. Others can see things you do not see or don't want to see.

If you do not acknowledge your limitations, you will not seek solutions for them. When you try to do everything yourself, you prevent others from moving toward you. It's important that you accept and respect the anointing in others, because that anointing longs to become necessary to you.

Principle No. 6
Announce your dream to others

Your dream should be too big for you alone, so you will need to announce it to others (See 2 Chronicles 2:5). If your dream is not big enough to consume you, it will not move you. When you announce your dream to others it will:

- Energize and encourage those that are with you.

- Inspire creativity in others' ideas.

- Cause those who oppose you to decide to join you.

- Cause those who disagree with you secretly to be forced to reveal themselves to you publicly.

- Make it more difficult to fail.

Principle No. 7
Consult other uncommon achievers (see 2 Chron. 2:3)

Uncommon achievers will invest whatever is necessary to learn the secrets of others. Uncommon achievers treasure every moment they are in the presence of greatness. Uncommon achievers will conduct themselves wisely in the presence of greatness. Uncommon achievers have uncommon expectations of others.

Uncommon achievers often discern true motives and attitudes before you ever open your mouth.

Principle No. 8
Develop a plan for achieving your goals

Your plan is a written picture of your goals. It will eliminate the wrong people from your schedule. Planning always reveals the shortest route to your goal.

Principle No. 9
Always listen to both sides before making a decision (See Proverbs 1:5)

A wise man will hear, and will increase learning; and a man of understanding shall attain unto wise counsels.

Principle No. 10
Succeed at being you

Self-rejection and self-hatred are the root causes of many relationship problems. Know who you are and understand what kind of relationship you have with God, with yourself and with your fellowman. Rejecting ourselves just multiplies our problems. But self-acceptance will cause us to deal with the realities about ourselves.

It's important that we see ourselves as successful people. Nevertheless, true continued success comes from hearing God's voice (see John 10:27 and Isaiah 30:21).

Principle No. 11
Be determined that you will not live below the blessing that God has provided for you

We offer God whatever we have, and He gives us what He has. He takes all of our sins, faults, weaknesses and failures and gives us His ability, His righteousness and His strength. He takes our poverty and gives us His riches. He takes our diseases and sicknesses, and gives us His healing and health. He takes our messed up, failure-filled past and gives us His hope of a bright future.

Principle No. 12
Don't Get in a Hurry!

Solomon refused to hurry. He took the time necessary to develop essential relationships with kings, skilled craftsmen, and thousands of workers.

Here are some facts that will help you deal with hurrying.

- When you hurry, you increase the mistakes you make (Gen 16:1-4).

- When you hurry, you often have to redo everything you have done.

- When you slow down, you follow the example of other uncommon achievers.

- Slowing down provides time to receive worthy counsel.

- One moment of hurry can create one month of chaos.

As you read through the following chapters of this book, you will find that the habits outlined will be carefully drawn from these principles of success. I encourage you to be a doer of the Word and not a hearer only.

Determine to put these principles into practice in your daily life. As you do, it won't be long before you'll discover that you've developed good habits, success habits that will set you on a course of greater prosperity and blessing than you've ever before imagined. May God's blessings be upon you richly as you succeed in becoming an uncommon achiever!

Pastor Greg Powe
Senior Pastor
Revealing Truth Ministries

Chapter 1

Understand The Importance of Your Own Success

Do you realize that someone's life depends upon your success? Too often we accept failure because we don't understand how important it is to God for us to succeed. It is absolutely essential that you and I get a hold of the importance of our success. This includes success on every front—in everything that God has called us to do.

After Joshua received God's call on his life, the Lord began to prepare him to take Moses' place. God said, "Be strong and of a good courage: for unto this people shalt thou divide for an inheritance the land, which I sware unto their fathers to give them" (Josh. 1:6).

God told Joshua, "I want you to be strong and I want you to be courageous, so you can fulfill a promise that I made to this people."

This also applies to your own life and your own success. Have you ever considered that somebody's eternal destiny is tied to your own personal success?

You may never realize that you were a failure to a particular individual until you get to heaven and find out that this person had been appointed by God to follow you as you followed Christ. During that season of time, you had stopped following Christ, and, unknowingly, you failed this individual.

Each one of us has far greater influence than we realize. Every living soul has influence. Whether you are influencing people positively or negatively is based upon who you are in Christ. That's why it's so essential to stay on course and not falter in your walk before God.

Therefore, don't go off course. You're not going to be successful if you don't stay on course. You can't be up today and down tomorrow and expect success to come to you. What if the person called to follow you last week happened to be watching you on one of your down days? What did that person witness? It was the day that you just felt as if you had a right to go off. It also happened to be the very day that individual needed you to be an example of endurance, perseverance and patience.

> *God told Joshua, "Only be thou strong and very courageous, that thou mayest observe to do according to all the law, which Moses my servant commanded thee: turn not from it to*

*the right hand or to the left, that thou mayest
prosper whithersoever thou goest."*

—Joshua 1:7

Accept the Help You Need to Succeed

In all that you do, for each and every day of your life, God
wants you to prosper. He desires that you succeed in all that
concerns you. There are some things you're good at, and there
are other things that you do less well. There are also some things
that you just plain stink at. For those things you cannot do, God's
got someone waiting on the sidelines to come in and help you.
Therefore, you can always succeed, even in the matters for which
you are not particularly gifted.

Pride can sometimes get in your way, making you feel reluctant
to reach for the help you need to be whole and experience success.
And that's one of the principles that we're going to investigate:
nobody knows everything.

The Bible says:

*This book of the law shall not depart out of
thy mouth.*

—Joshua 1:8

Notice for a moment what God did not say. He didn't say
that this book of the law would flip and fall off of your coffee table
onto your living room floor. Rather, God expects that the words
of the Bible will be found in your mouth. This point is vitally

important. He didn't even say that the words of this book should be in your head. He said, "in your mouth."

Furthermore, God said that they shouldn't depart out of your mouth. Why did He say this? Consider this: when you open your mouth, whatever is in your mouth comes out. Only what's *in* your mouth comes *out* of your mouth. So, the only thing that should be in your mouth is the Word of God.

The Bible says,

> *This book of the law shall not depart out of thy mouth; but thou shalt meditate therein day and night.*
>
> —Joshua 1:8

To *meditate* on God's Word day and night means *to mutter* over it. In other words, rehearse it over and over and over and over. Just keep repeating it to yourself. Why is this important? Because, just as with practicing a lay-up shot on the basketball court or a particular swing in tennis, what you're rehearsing or practicing is what will come forth in your moment of challenge.

Succeed on Purpose

Are you tired of failing? Are you tired of experiencing shortcomings? Are you tired of shooting for the stars and not even getting off the launching pad? Well, know this: success is not an accident. You are not going to be successful by chance. If you're successful, it will be on purpose, because you purposed within yourself to succeed. Failure operates in a similar fashion.

When we fail, we fail on purpose. You are the one who determines your own success.

Joshua 1:8 continues:

> *This book of the law shall not depart out of thy mouth; but thou shalt meditate therein day and night, that thou mayest observe to do according to all that is written therein: for then thou shalt make thy way prosperous and then thou shalt have good success.*

You're going to make your own way prosperous. It's not your momma's fault. It's not your daddy's fault. It's not your uncle's fault. It's not the church's fault. It's not God's fault. It's not the devil's fault. It's not your teacher's fault. If you are not successful, it's your own fault. He said *you* make your own way prosperous.

You're not going to be able to make your way prosperous if you don't know how. Nevertheless, God promises the powerful blessing of "good success" to you and to me. He also promises to go with us every step of the way to help us make success happen.

> *Have not I commanded thee? Be strong and of a good courage; be not afraid, neither be thou dismayed: for the Lord thy God is with thee whithersoever thou goest.*
>
> —Joshua 1:9

In this passage of Scripture, God is saying, "I'm here with you to make sure that every word is maximized and every word produces exactly what I want it to produce in the way in which it should."

Do you really believe that God is with you everywhere you go — that He's not merely a spectator in the affairs and events of your life? He's there to make sure everything He promised you can be manifested in your life through you. He oversees every word that's in your mouth—the same words that flow out of your mouth.

Why does God carefully watch every word you say? He does so because your success is vital to His plans and purposes on this earth. Your success has impact and influence and is enormously important. Therefore, your first success principle is this: never underestimate the importance of your own success!

Four Objectives for Your Success

Success is a powerful soul-winning tool. Do you want your business to grow? Do you want your church to grow? Do you want whatever you're doing to grow? Do you want to prosper? If so, then be successful. Then take your success a step further to uncommon achievement. The study of Solomon's success will help us to achieve four objectives.

The first one is as follows:

1. To show you how to become an uncommon achiever.

Expect to become an uncommon achiever. Too many individuals have become too satisfied with being average.

That's not you. God intends for you to rise far above the norm, so get ready!

Objective number two is as follows:

2. *To show you that you have to stand when others have fallen.*

I'm convinced that there's a key, a secret that allows some to maintain while everyone around them seems to falter and collapse. When you look at the world's economy you will always notice that at the same time that some individuals are falling, others seem to be doing more than ever before. It's an amazing fact. One person is barely making it while another person is accomplishing more than he or she ever thought or dreamed possible. Sometimes both people live in the same neighborhood. They might even sit right next to each other in the same church pew every Sunday. Have you ever wondered why this is so? There has got to be a reason.

The third objective is a powerful statement regarding attitude:

3. *To show you how to be encouraging when others criticize.*

You need to learn how to be encouraging and how to stay encouraging regardless of how critical others become. With the power of this attitude, folks will look forward to being around you. They'll feel as if they can't wait to get into your presence because they know that there's something coming out of you that excites them. People feel encouraged just being near you.

This is the power of attitude—and we've got to learn how to obtain it. When you have it people will gravitate towards you and will just attach themselves to you, because they realize that there's something uncommon about you. They see something in you as an asset. This powerful attitude will cause folks to follow you to church. They'll look at you and see where you attend church, and they'll say, "I want some of that!"

The fourth objective will also make you stand out in a crowd:

4. *To teach you how to thrust forward when others are sitting down.*

I believe that these principles will take you from poverty to plenty, from disillusionment into uncommon confidence. This is the kind of confidence that is unshaken when all of the evidence in the natural says you ought to be scared, fearful and about to lose it. Despite the circumstances around you, you have uncommon confidence. With this attitude, when somebody's telling you that you ought to shut down your business, you turn around and open up another one.

If you get a hold of these principles to grab them and receive them as your own, you will find that it's very difficult—if not impossible—for you to fail. You will have a guaranteed success rate of 100 percent! If every church member would apply these principles to his or her life from this day forward, I believe that we would see a success rate of 100 percent in everything we are seeking to accomplish for the glory of God.

Conclusion

There are many highly successful individuals in the Bible, but Solomon is one of the most successful of all. We're going to use Solomon's life as a model to draw out biblical habits of success.

These habits will assist you as you deal with various business issues and as you deal with your family. They will help you with anything at which you want to be successful. These habits will work in any arena of your life.

You can begin to achieve and walk in your vitally important success by beginning to understand the power of attitude. Turn over and let's take a look at this next powerful habit that can start you on the pathway of success.

Chapter 2

Discover The Power Of Attitude

Attitude is a vital principle for your success, for attitude equals power. The right attitude is a key that can begin unlocking great doors of success in your life.

Inheriting the promises that God has for you will require an entirely new attitude. Not only will you need a new attitude to unlock the door to your own blessings in God, but your new attitude will cause others to reap their inheritances, as well. Your attitude has the power to make things happen.

Let's take a look at this in the Word of God. The Amplified version of Joshua reads as follows:

Be strong (confident) and of good courage, for you shall cause this people to inherit the land which I swore to their fathers to give them.

Only you be strong and very courageous, that you may do according to all the law which Moses My servant commanded you. Turn not from it to the right hand or to the left, that you may prosper wherever you go.

This Book of the Law shall not depart out of your mouth, but you shall meditate on it day and night, that you may observe and do according to all that is written in it. For then you shall make your way prosperous, and then you shall deal wisely and have good success.

> *Have not I commanded you? Be strong, vigorous, and very courageous. Be not afraid, neither be dismayed, for the Lord your God is with you wherever you go.*
> —Joshua 1:6-9, (AMP)

God commanded Joshua and the Israelites to gain a certain attitude. It was an attitude of strength, courage, boldness and fearlessness.

I believe that heaven will be filled with people with great attitudes. No one up there will be negative. You won't hear negative folks walking around complaining, "I think there's too much gold around here." "I don't see why they had to put all this gold everywhere." "I don't even like gold anyway."

Down here we run into these negative people all of the time. Someone always seems to be voicing an opinion about something they don't like. You've heard it. You ask these individuals, "Why don't you come to church with me?" They respond, "Well, I don't want to go to your church because it's too big."

Such statements can leave you wondering, *What you desire then is that everything stay small, which means you want to attend a church where there's no growth. And no growth means that there are more people going to hell than going to heaven.*

These individuals say, "I want to go to a little church so I can feel loved." This attitude doesn't come from God. When do unbelievers attempt to crash a party where no one else showed up? Do they ever go to an empty club just to sit around and talk to the bartender and waitress? Of course not! When people go to a club they attend because they feel, "Man, it's happening there."

So, why would the same individuals seek out a church with a small congregation? It makes no sense. You will feel loved where you sense the moving of the Holy Spirit, and that's a church that will be full of life, activity and people.

Your success flies on the wings of your attitude. A great attitude will take you higher and give you altitude. A sour, griping, negative attitude will have the opposite effect.

God desired for the Israelites to gain success, which is why He addressed their attitude. God was providing the Israelites with a principle or key for their success. If they obeyed, they could be certain that He would make their way prosperous and successful. They would become uncommon achievers.

Solomon the Uncommon Achiever

Solomon was an uncommon achiever. Uncommon achievers are different, for in a world full of doubt, they believe. When people all around them are doubting, uncommon achievers continue to hold fast in their faith. In a quitting world, they persevere. When everybody else wants to quit, uncommon achievers find one more reason to keep going. They dig deep within themselves and find the motivation to stay the course.

That's the reason I've told my congregation for years that I will not quit; therefore, I cannot be defeated. Why not make that your own personal motto? You will not quit; therefore, you will not be defeated.

In my life, I've got a very simple plan. I feel that if nothing else works for me, then I'll just merely wear out the devil with my persistent presence. He knows that I'm not going away. Regardless of what he tries to throw at me, like the Terminator, I'll be back. Do you remember that movie? This character was completely blown up with nothing remaining but his little arm. Nevertheless, he kept trying to accomplish his mission.

Solomon was not a perfect man, but he was a productive man. Because we're not yet perfect, sometimes we allow our own imperfections to make us believe that we'll never be productive. But look at what Solomon did. By today's standards, the temple that Solomon built would be valued in the neighborhood of $500 billion—not million but billion.

A billion dollars is impossible for many of us to fathom. We think it's a little more than a million dollars. But if you stacked up thousand dollar bills in a pile twelve inches high, it would equal a million dollars. But $1 billion would be a stack of thousand dollar bills as tall as the Empire State Building. That's quite a difference, isn't it?

So now when you read in the Wall Street Journal that a particular company is worth billions, you'll have a little better idea of just what that means. That's why it doesn't bother some companies or some billionaires to lose a few million here or there. Depending upon how much you have, a million dollars can seem like the change that you and I keep in the ashtrays of our cars.

Solomon was an uncommon producer. Not only did he build God's house, but he constructed an incredible house for himself, as well. Solomon's house was awesome!

Success is like everything else; it requires a plan. So what's your plan for success? How big is that plan? How successful do you want to be? I can guarantee you that what you fail to plan you'll never achieve. If you don't have a plan, you won't get there. If for some reason you do land on your feet, you won't be able to stay there because you won't understand where you are. Genuine success requires a plan, and that plan must include all that concerns you—your house, your family, your children, your business and your ministry.

What Solomon Wanted Most

One of the most distinguishing traits of Solomon is what he desired more than anything else in life. Let's take a look at what that was. 1 Kings 3:5 says,

In Gibeon the Lord appeared to Solomon in a dream by night: and God said, Ask what I shall give thee.

What a question! A lot of us would have missed it if God had ever asked us this question. We might be tempted to ask God for a Mercedes Benz. Often we're not successful because our thinking hasn't expanded beyond what things we can see. We have an opportunity to accomplish great things and to receive great things, but we don't dream high enough. We need to look a little deeper at our dreams.

You need to have a dream. Each one of us needs to have a dream or a vision—something that we desire to obtain. God asked Solomon, "What shall I give thee?" How would you respond if this happened to you? If you need to tell God, "Well, let me go pray about it," then you're not ready.

Imagine someone walked up to you today and said, "God has laid it on my heart to finance your business plan, so let me see it."

You've been asking the Lord to give you your own business for the last ten years. God finally sends somebody to finance your business plan. That individual says, "Give it to me." If you don't have a business plan to place in his hands at that very moment, then you're not ready.

Maybe you do have a plan, but it's something you scrawled on the back of a piece of used notebook paper that no one can read but you. Don't expect that to produce success. Your plan will succeed only to the degree of effort that you put into it. Even if you put great effort into it, perhaps the only thing your effort will produce is that it got your plan noticed.

Let's look again at this passage.

> *God said, Ask what I shall give thee. And*
> *Solomon said...*
>
> —1 Kings 3:5-6

Notice that Solomon didn't skip a beat. He didn't stutter, and he didn't need to run and find a prophet to tell him how to respond. Why? Because Solomon already had something in him. Let's look at Solomon's response.

And Solomon said,

> *Thou hast shown unto thy servant David my*
> *father great mercy, according as he walked*
> *before thee in truth, and in righteousness, and*
> *in uprightness of heart with thee; and thou*
> *hast kept for him. And now...*
>
> —1 Kings 3:6-7

The first thing that you notice about Solomon's vision is that it was not selfish. His vision was connected to another man—his father. The Bible says, "And if ye have not been faithful in that which is another man's, who shall give you that which is your own?" (Luke 16:12).

Seeing Beyond Yourself

One of the reasons many of you have problems obtaining success the way God desires it for you is that no one would benefit from your success but you. Your accomplishments would be selfish. But God is seeking those whose thinking is a little broader than that. He's looking for those in whom He can invest and receive a return from His investment. He seeks to bless those who will, in turn, become a blessing to thousands and even millions of others. Or, it may be that only one other person will be blessed through you, but that individual will turn around and bless millions of others.

As is often the case, one individual ministered into Billy Graham's life. The result of that person's ministry was enormous. Thank God that person was obedient to do what God said, for that obedience produced the results witnessed in this powerful evangelist's ministry.

What if that person had responded, "Lord, can I do something bigger than that?" One act of obedience produced one of the greatest evangelists of all time and is responsible for millions of people saved and on their way to heaven. One lowly act of obedience brought honor to the kingdom of God and integrity to the ministry of the gospel. That's great success!

But in modern thinking, few of us see it like that. Today, we have individuals working in the children's ministry who are consumed with a desire to get somewhere else and be noticed for what they're doing. Therefore, they overlook the little child who may grow up to be another Billy Graham.

Solomon's desires, dreams and success were directly connected to the promise that God had made to his father—his father's heart's desire.

Maintaining a Humble Heart While Seeking Favor

Do you want to please the Lord and obtain His favor in your life? If so, learn to approach God in the attitude of humility that Solomon used. Let's look.

> *And now, O Lord my God, thou hast made thy servant king instead of David my father and I am but a little child: I know not how to go out or come in.*
>
> —1 Kings 3:7

Solomon tells God, "I don't know how to do this." He was not fully mature yet, but he still had a dream, and he still had a desire. He was still productive. He said:

> *And thy servant is in the midst of thy people which thou hast chosen, a great people, that cannot be numbered nor counted for multitude. Give therefore thy servant an understanding heart.*
>
> —1 Kings 3:8-9

The very first thing that Solomon asked for was a hearing heart. He told God, "Lord, I want to know how to hear from you. That's what I want to know. No, I don't need the money yet."

Most people would say, "Lord, if I can just get the money." They sit around praying, "Lord send me investors." But the Lord is saying, "Well, get something for them to invest in!"

Solomon said:

> *...to judge thy people...*
>
> —1 Kings 3:9

Solomon didn't want a hearing heart just for his own benefit and for his own profit. He wanted a hearing heart or an understanding heart so that he could be more effective in his calling to God's people. His entire purpose revolved around them. He said:

> *...that I may discern between good and bad: for who is able to judge this thy so great a people?*
>
> —1 Kings 3:9

Solomon's prayer to God reveals great humility. And God promises to promote the humble (See 1 Peter 5:5).

The passage continues:

> *And the speech pleased the Lord.*
>
> —1 Kings 3:10

Do you want to please the Lord? If so, then talk like Solomon. Approach God as Solomon did, and God will be pleased, and with His pleasure comes great rewards. Let's look.

> *And the speech pleased the Lord, that Solomon had asked this thing. And God said unto him, Because thou hast asked this thing, and hast not asked for thyself long life; neither...*
>
> —1 Kings 3:10-11

God was impressed at what Solomon *didn't* ask for, and that's important. God said that he didn't ask for a long life, because that shouldn't be the most important thing to us. It doesn't really matter how long we live if our lives don't count for something in God's kingdom. Some individual's long lives are little more than an extended opportunity for Satan to cause them to miss heaven. They're here doing nothing and therefore apt to turn more people away from God than towards Him.

Make your life count for something on this earth, for your life matters greatly to God. You're not an island or an isolated creature. What you do has a powerful impact on the rest of the body of Christ, and that's serious business.

> *And the speech pleased the Lord, that Solomon had asked this thing. And God said unto him, Because thou hast asked this thing, and has not asked for thyself long life; neither hast asked riches for thyself.*
>
> —1 Kings 3:10-11

Notice, he didn't ask riches for himself. That's another thing about financial wealth and prosperity: when you learn how to be successful, it will come to you. You won't have to chase it. Money will follow your success. As a matter of fact, money pursues success; so become successful at something and the money will follow.

This truth applies whether you're saved or unsaved. Even ungodly men and women who become the best at what they do end up being paid very well. Look at our nation's best athletes. They became successful in the areas in which they were gifted, and prosperity followed that success. They didn't seek money, wealth and fame. Instead, they pursued excellence in their gifts, and prosperity followed. God said,

> *...neither hast asked riches for thyself, nor hast asked the life of thine enemies.*
>
> —1 Kings 3:11

Solomon didn't ask God for anything that most of us would think might make us successful. Most of us think that if we only just didn't have enemies, we'd be able to shine. We think, "If it just wasn't these people coming against me. Lord, just wipe out my in-laws. Just get rid of everybody who's ever disagreed with me." Having no enemies will not ensure your success. Too often we use our enemies as a point of blame for our own personal failures.

God spoke about what Solomon asked that pleased Him:

> *...but hast asked for thyself understanding to discern judgment; Behold, I have done according to thy words: lo, I have given thee a wise and an understanding heart; so that there was none like thee before thee, neither after thee shall any arise like unto thee. And I have also given thee that which thou hast not asked, both riches, and honour: So that there shall*

*not be any among the kings like unto thee all
thy days.*

—1 Kings 3:11-13

Because Solomon asked God for a wise and understanding heart, God gave it to him. But God didn't stop there. He added to that all the things that Solomon could have requested but did not. Solomon's priorities were right before God. Therefore, God blessed him with more wealth and power than any other king who ever reigned in Israel.

What was the power that unlocked that incredible blessing in his life? It was the power of attitude. Solomon's attitude of selflessness, humility and right priorities opened the door to privilege, wealth and power that was beyond his greatest dream or expectation. Your right attitude can do the same for you!

Let's turn now and look at another powerful habit for your success—it is the ability to dream and to dream big. In order to become successful, you must become a dreamer. Turn the page over and let me explain.

Chapter 3

Dare to Dream Big

Solomon built the temple of God—one of the greatest structures ever made by human hands—because he was a man who knew how to dream and how to dream big. Solomon was a man of vision and he was a dreamer. What about you?

Our culture and our society have killed our dreams. Today, few of us even remember how to dream. We just go to work and return home to eat and watch a little television before we prepare to repeat the whole thing all over again. We don't have any desires, any special plans or anything we've decided to do that will make our lives better and more meaningful.

As a matter of fact, most people don't even work for themselves. They work for someone else in order to pay their bills, at least until they begin to realize that this may not be God's best plan for their lives.

Now, Solomon was an uncommon achiever who accomplished some things that no one else has since. In his time, without the help of machines, electricity, computers or investors, Solomon managed the building of a $500 billion project that dazzled the ancient world and would dazzle us,; as well,; if it were still standing.

Solomon was a dreamer who had the ability to dream and dream big. What about you? Are you a dreamer? Or, have you long ago lost your ability to dream? Every individual needs to have a dream, a vision and a goal. You should have a vision for your life, your family, your work, your financial prosperity and your future. Your dream or dreams should be things that you want to obtain or achieve during the course of your life.

Your dream may not personally affect you, and it doesn't have to. Your goal may involve providing a better future for your children, which is a great goal for parents. You may tell yourself, "I want to make sure my children have a better opportunity to succeed in life than I had. And I'm going to personally do what I can to make sure that I provide them that opportunity." If that's your dream, it's a good one.

Don't sit back and passively wait for the government to provide your children with opportunities. Determine that you will hear from God on their behalf and do everything in your power to make sure that they have the opportunities for success that you never enjoyed.

The Power of a Dream

David made that decision concerning his son Solomon. With all of his heart, David desired to build a temple for God. Nevertheless, God would not permit him to do so because he was a man with blood on his hands. He had been a bloody warrior throughout his entire lifetime, and God wanted a man of peace to build His temple.

Did David lose interest in his dream because God said no? Did he just forget about it? Absolutely not! Instead, he said, "Okay, Lord, I'm going to provide everything for my son to build You a house. I'm going to raise my son with the objective in his heart to build You a house."

David was a dreamer, so he placed his dream into the heart of his son.

Dreamers provide jobs and income for those who refuse to dream. You may right now be working for someone who dared to dream. If that individual hadn't been a dreamer, you might not have a job today. So be grateful for that person who was courageous enough to dream. Better yet, dream yourself. Who knows how many people are waiting to benefit from the power of your dream.

Dreamers stretch the imaginations of everyone around them. When you come into the presence of a dreamer, he or she will make you bigger. Dreamers thrust average people into the zone of greatness. That's the power of a dream.

Nevertheless, as with everything else in life that is truly worthwhile, dreamers are also often challenged to pay a great price for their dreams. Those around them who cannot understand their dream, or who have themselves lost the ability to dream, often paint them as money hungry, greedy and materialistic. Just remember that the more worthwhile your dream, the greater the price that may be exacted from you. But when you finally realize your dream, the reward will be well worth the price.

Your Dream Defines You

Deborah and I came to Tampa with a dream. But when I arrived, I had to start where almost everyone starts— at the bottom, alone, with little more than my dream. When I came to Tampa I had just enough to feed my family.

I started out working as a car salesman at Courtesy Pontiac. That's where I worked until I got a better job as an executive housekeeper, which is a fancy name for a janitor. I stripped and waxed floors, while all the time, I had a dream inside of me.

I didn't let my present occupation define who I was. Instead, I was defined by what God called me to do. I had to do a lot of things on the way to the fulfillment of my dream, but I never stopped dreaming just because I was selling cars. That was simply what I had to do as a means to an end. I needed to bring home the bacon — and a little fried chicken every now and then.

Uncommon achievers do not allow present circumstances to rob them of their dreams. The desire to achieve the dream that they nurture and maintain deep inside can stand up to the test of the trip. A dreamer's desire will keep while he or she goes through the steps needed along the way to the dream's fulfillment.

Some people call dreamers materialistic, money hungry, money grubbing and a lot of other slanderous names. But if you're successful at what you do then you will eventually become rich. Wealth will follow your success, and it doesn't really matter what you do. If you're successful at anything, you will eventually acquire wealth. That's one reason that Satan doesn't want you to be successful. He much prefers that you be powerless and broke.

You can enjoy success in any walk of life. I've witnessed this phenomenon in an individual who simply started off doing little more than cutting grass—just mowing a neighbor's lawn. Before long he was cutting grass for all of the neighbors. Eventually, he was cutting grass for an entire subdivision.

The day came when this successful person hired others to work for him because he had too much grass to cut by himself. While he was cutting, some homeowners asked if he could plant flowers as well. He also began to put in sprinkler systems.

Before he was finished, this individual owned a multi-million dollar landscaping business. All of it grew out of one person's success at cutting grass. A dream was born from small beginnings, which is often where dreams start.

What Is Your Dream?

Solomon knew what he wanted to do, and he developed a passion for his dreams. When God told Solomon He would give him anything he asked, as we saw earlier, Solomon didn't skip a beat. He knew exactly what he wanted.

That's because Solomon had a dream inside of him. Let's look at Solomon's response.

And Solomon said, Thou hast shown unto thy servant David my father great mercy, according as he walked before thee in truth, and in righteousness, and in uprightness of heart with thee; and thou hast kept for him this great kindness, that thou hast given him a son to sit on his throne, as it is this day. And now...

—1 Kings 3:6-7

When God granted Solomon anything he wanted as king, the young man didn't have to consult a prophet. He knew what he wanted and what he needed. Solomon asked God for wisdom, which he later used to build a great temple for God—that was his dream.

What is your dream? Do you know what you want today? Or are you just sitting around hoping that things will get better?

Nothing can get better for you until you decide what better is. Personally, I am not waiting to see how things are going to turn out in my life. God's Word already assures me that everything will turn out well. Therefore, I must set my course in order to achieve my goals. I've got to make decisions that will bring to fulfillment what I desire to see happen in my life.

Birthing Your Dream

Your dream must be birthed, and it cannot be borrowed. You cannot live your life based upon another person's dream. So think creatively. Don't let discouragement tell you there's nothing new coming for you. There will be if you dare to dream.

You know, around 1932 a certain politician proposed shutting down the patent office. This man became convinced that keeping the office open was a waste of time and money because everything that could ever be invented had already been thought of. Can you imagine how narrow a thinker that man must have been? He had lost his ability to think creatively and to dream, but don't you ever lose yours.

Are you presently doing the same thing you've done for years? Have you ever considered asking God for wisdom to do what you do better? Think creatively. How can you make what you do every day better? Your better ideas can make you a millionaire.

Someone made millions by twisting a wire up and creating a paper clip — just a little something to hold papers together.

Do you use Post-It Notes? These handy little sticky notes were actually created by accident, and they became a multi-million dollar idea.

Ask yourself this question: What would you attempt to do if you knew it was absolutely impossible to fail? What would you attempt to do if time was not a factor, education was not an issue and you had all the money you needed? Given these parameters, what comes to mind?

That's the thing you should be striving to do; that's your dream. It's what you should be striving for, even if you've been told that it's an impossibility. The Bible says, "For with God nothing shall be impossible" (Luke 1:37).

You may need some encouragement from others to get motivated to start your dream, but eventually your dream will motivate others to follow you. Therefore, it's vital that you surround yourself with the right people who can inspire and instruct you; and who can encourage you when you encounter resistance, which will happen.

Your heart may be filled with your dream, but you also realize that there's a little fear in there, as well. There's also a little intimidation because of the greatness of your dream. That's why it's important to have those around you who can tell you, "Go ahead, you can do it. Come on, let's go do this thing. Let's go get it done-I'm with you all the way."

At first, their encouragement will help pull you along, but before long you will be leading them. God has sent them to you at the beginning to help jump-start your vision.

Uncommon Desire and Uncommon Dreams

To launch an uncommon dream you must have uncommon desire. Solomon had a desire to do what had never been done before, and the fruit of his uncommon desire was the building of a $500 billion temple for God. If you have a desire to build a dream, then feed that desire until it becomes an obsession. Go to sleep at night thinking about the thing you desire to accomplish for God.

Your dream must be important enough to cause you to change your daily routine. If your dream is not important enough to you for you to change your daily routine, you'll never accomplish it. This is one reason that most people never move beyond average to become uncommon achievers.

What you've been doing up to today has produced what you have today. If you want to produce more, accomplish greater things or be a part of something greater, you've got to change your daily routine.

A God Idea

Let God place the dream that He has for you into your heart. Pray and ask Him for it. All the money in the world will not do you any good if you don't have God's dream in your heart. You may even be able to get a bank to finance your idea if it looks good enough. You can talk people into financing a bad idea if you are a smooth talker. But you won't be genuinely fulfilled in your life unless you have God ideas, and God ideas come out of the heart of God. So, ask Him to show you a dream and to birth it deep within you, and like Solomon, you'll be taking a vital step to becoming an uncommon achiever.

Chapter 4

Make Wisdom
Your Obsession

Solomon was one of the greatest kings who ever reigned on earth. He was one of the wisest, wealthiest, most powerful and influential men who ever lived. But the secret to his amazing success was wisdom. Wisdom was his obsession, and once he obtained it, wealth, power, privilege, favor and great influence followed. Therefore, a major key to your success is making wisdom your obsession.

The Bible reveals how it was that wisdom became the key to Solomon's success. So, let's look at 1 Kings 3:7:

> *And now, O Lord my God, thou hast made thy*
> *servant king instead of David my father and I*
> *am but a little child: I know not how to go out*
> *or to come in.*

When God came to Solomon and promised to bless him with anything he could ask, the one and only thing Solomon requested was wisdom. But this passage of Scripture shows us why. Solomon didn't start out being wise. As a matter of fact, he tells God how unwise he is.

He says, *"I don't know how to start, and I don't know how to end."* Have you ever been in that position? You know what it is that God called you to do, but you don't know how to get started, and you don't know how to carry it through to completion. You have a great vision, but you don't even know how to get started.

Some people know how to start things, and they initiate projects continually, but they don't complete them. The Bible says:

> *For which of you, intending to build a tower,*
> *sitteth not down first, and countest the cost,*
> *whether he have sufficient to finish it? Lest*
> *haply, after he hath laid the foundation, and*
> *is not able to finish it, all that behold it begin*
> *to mock him, Saying, This man began to build,*
> *and was not able to finish.*
> —Luke 14:28-30

A lot of people start things, but they don't ever finish anything. My mission in life is to finish and to finish strong. I don't want to just finish with a little whimper.

Make it your intention to have greater influence in the end of your life than at the beginning. Desire to have greater power and greater anointing at the end than at the beginning! That's my goal. As a matter of fact, I plan on being more anointed tomorrow than I am today. Not only do I plan for it, but I also expect it and am looking forward to it.

I'm going to do everything I know to do to make my tomorrow better than my today. Make it your goal to stay focused on getting better, and you will finish strong.

Some individuals will feel happy if they finish at all, while others want to finish strong. These are the successful ones—those who want to finish first, who want to be number one.

Solomon told God in 1 Kings 3:7-8:

> *I know not how to go out or come in. And thy servant is in the midst of thy people which thou hast chosen, a great people, that cannot be numbered nor counted for multitude.*

How many people do you believe God wants you to influence with the anointing that He's placed upon your life? Your assignment from God is to influence everyone with whom you come into contact every day.

You are Called to Be a Person of Influence

How many people have you actually influenced? You are anointed by God if you've been born again. So what are you doing with that anointing? The anointing of God involves your influence. Who are you influencing, and what is the outcome of your influence? Are the people who come into contact with you better off or worse off because of you?

I'm not suggesting that some day you will become more anointed, and then you'll have influence. You may become more anointed, but you are anointed already. What are you doing with the anointing that you presently have?

In this passage of scripture, we see that Solomon was concerned about the great multitude of people he was called to influence. His response to that multitude was to cry out to God for wisdom. He didn't say, "I need money. I need an army so that I can beat them into submission." No, Solomon said, "I need wisdom."

Most people fail or fall short of accomplishing God's highest level of success — which is His perfect will for them — because they lack wisdom. They speak about things that they should remain silent about; they get angry when they should take a walk and cool off, or perhaps they quit their jobs when it wasn't God's time for them to go. They may complain, "They weren't treating me right, there!" Nevertheless, there was something they did have to teach at that job that was never imparted because that individual left.

In this passage, Solomon reveals one of the main reasons that members of the body of Christ fall short of the anointing and power that we ought to display according to the Bible. Because we've fallen short so often, we've lost our ability to have the influence in which God intended for us to walk.

Unbelievers should look at us and want to be like us. They ought to observe us from afar and want to be around us. That's a wealthy place to walk in, and we're on our way there. That's the kind of anointing Solomon had on him.

As God's people, we are, indeed, on our way to a wealthy place. But we need to ask ourselves whether, when we get there, will we also be able to stay there? And once we get there, will we recognize it for what it really is? It will take God's wisdom for us to correctly answer such questions. Let's look again at Solomon's response:

> *Give therefore thy servant an understanding heart [or a hearing heart] to judge thy people.*

Solomon asked for an understanding, or a hearing, heart. He requested what was necessary in order to serve the people of God. That's probably part of the problem for most people. When they go to God, they're looking for something to benefit themselves, not something to benefit others. The anointing on your life is not for you. The anointing on your life is for others. Greg Powe is not anointed for Greg Powe; he's anointed for those to whom he's called to minister.

The passage continues,

> *Give therefore thy servant an understanding heart to judge thy people, that I may discern between good and bad.*
> —1 Kings 3:9

There are a lot of people who genuinely don't know the difference between good and bad, especially with respect to relationships and selecting those with whom they establish close relationships. Whom you surround yourself with will largely determine what you desire, as we'll see in greater detail later on.

Your relationships impact what you believe you should strive to achieve.

Solomon said:

> *...that I may discern between good and bad: for who is able to judge this thy so great a people? And the speech...*
> —1 Kings 3:9-10

Your People are a Great People

Notice Solomon's humility in this passage. Although he's been placed over the entire nation as king, he doesn't see himself as greater than his subjects. He speaks to God about the greatness of the people he's been called to lead. Solomon didn't consider those he was called to rule as beneath him or inferior to him.

Instead, he tells God, "You have a great people, God, whom You've called me to lead. This is a great job. This is a great task. But I'm not equipped in myself to do the job. Therefore, I need Your wisdom."

Do you think you could raise your children better if you had the wisdom of God? The reason why you've had so many problems with your children is that you may be trying to raise them without God's wisdom.

The passage continues:

> *For who is able to judge this thy so great a people? And the speech pleased the Lord, that Solomon had asked this thing.*
>
> —1 Kings 3:9-10

Notice that Solomon's request pleased the Lord:

> *And God said unto him, Because thou hast asked this thing, and hast not asked for thyself long life; neither hast asked riches for thyself, nor hast asked the life of thine enemies; but hast asked for thyself understanding to discern judgment; Behold, I have done according to thy words: lo, I have given thee a wise and an understanding heart; so that there was none like thee before thee, neither after thee shall any arise like unto thee.*
>
> —1 Kings 3:11-12

I believe if we grab hold of what this verse is telling us that, in our own time, God will do the same for us as He did for Solomon. God will bless us with wise and understanding hearts.

There's a divine assignment that God established before the foundation of the world just for you. It's the purpose for which you were created, and it's also the fulfillment of your deepest longings. Your success in life depends upon knowing and walking in that assignment.

One problem that occurs as people are being equipped for their purposes is they compare themselves among themselves, which is unwise. For each individual's calling is unique, requiring circumstances and opportunities that only God understands.

Nonetheless, God said that Solomon would be a person who couldn't be compared with anyone else, because he would rise so far above everyone else on earth. In order to launch him in his destiny, God gave Solomon great wisdom.

Let's see what else the Bible tells us comes with wisdom:

> *And I have also given thee that which thou hast not asked, both riches, and honour: so that there shall not be any among the kings like unto thee all thy days.*
>
> —1 Kings 3:13

Coming In Line for Riches and Honor

This passage shows us how to become wealthy people and how to receive great riches and honor. God shows us that these things follow wisdom. Get wisdom and you'll get riches and then honor. Get wisdom and you'll get these other things — and you won't even have to ask for them.

Don't waste a whole lot of time praying and begging for money, riches, cars, houses, expensive jewelry and other similar goods. In these verses, God says, "Get some wisdom. You get wisdom so that you can be successful in accomplishing what I've called you to do. Riches and honor will follow the wisdom. I'll see to it."

In response to Solomon's request for wisdom, God gave him a wise heart, but there was so much more to it than that. Often we consider that such events were instantaneous — *poof*, there it is! But is that how one receives wisdom? Just from where does wisdom come? Did God's giant hand reach down from heaven and touch Solomon's forehead to impart wisdom, so that Solomon instantly had all the wisdom he would ever need? That's what we may assume, but it's not how it happened.

The Bible reveals just how this impartation of wisdom took place in Solomon's life. Let's look at Ecclesiastes 1:12-13:

> *I the Preacher was king over Israel in Jerusalem. And I gave my heart to seek and search out by wisdom concerning all things...*

We see that God gave Solomon wisdom, but that didn't mean he wasn't required to study. It didn't imply that he didn't need to get in the Word to search out and seek out what it says. Just because you have wisdom from God does not mean that you just sit at home and ideas pop up in your head.

This passage of scripture says that Solomon gave his heart to seek and search out God's wisdom. He doesn't frantically seek and search in a foolish way. Rather, he conducts a search based upon the wisdom that God has imparted unto him. God's wisdom gives him the ability to seek and to search.

In other words, if Solomon was going to build a building, he wouldn't just start knocking together building materials and see how it turned out. He would use God's wisdom to find out what materials he would need to get started. Then he would seek through the places that had certain kinds of cedar and other particular types of wood and stone. Solomon would have used God's wisdom to seek out just the right kind of stone.

After he had found the stone he wanted to use, he would then begin searching for just the right person to cut the stone. It was this kind of careful wisdom that made him so successful.

God's Wisdom and Your Ministry

Has God called you to the ministry? Don't get too excited about that, for I'll let you in on a secret. He's called everybody into the ministry. As a matter of fact, the Word of God says this: "For many be called, but few chosen" (Matt. 20:16). Just because you have a calling on your life does not necessarily qualify you for success.

The assumption has been otherwise, especially in the old traditional church. Folks walk to the altar crying and sharing how the Lord just called them into the ministry. Everyone else surrounds them with great emotion. But such individuals may well get out there and fail, because there is so much they must learn before they step out into a successful ministry role. Many are called, but few are chosen.

Solomon was chosen. And afterward he said that he gave his heart to seek wisdom. To what have you given your heart? I can tell you to what you've given your heart. It's what you spend most of your time doing. If you spend the majority of your life and the majority of your time concentrating on your secular job, then your job owns your heart.

Let's say that you are a barber. If you are a successful barber, you will have to spend a certain amount of time cutting hair. Otherwise you will fail as a barber. It is the same with everything else in your life, too.

Some people go to law school, and they're deceived enough to think just because they get a law degree that they are now lawyers. The truth is that law school merely gave you a law degree. Now you are required to work hard at practicing law to be a successful attorney. The same is true with doctors and accountants and any other profession or line of work or ministry. Success requires a commitment of your heart, your time and your hard labor no matter what you do.

It may shock you to realize that most of us are *not* taught in school how to succeed. We're taught how to submit in life. We're trained to submit to other people's successes. The educational system does not teach you how to dream about having your own success. It teaches you how to submit to somebody else's dream and make him or her successful.

Let me explain the difference. School teaches you how to make money, but it doesn't teach you how to use money. It will teach you how to work for money, but it won't teach you how money works. A person who knows how to make money doesn't automatically understand how to make money work.

If you have a job, you know how to make money. But you may be completely ignorant about how to make money work. Therefore, you end up working for those individuals who understand how to make money work.

In God, you are on your way to a wealthy place, but you must remember that it's a place where you've never before been. It's where God wants you to live. But most church people never even consider that God wants them to operate in wealth. Nevertheless, Satan is well aware of how important wealth is for the successful completion of the mission that Jesus left us. The church of Jesus Christ has been commissioned with taking the gospel message to the four corners of the globe. But we're not going anywhere broke. Without financial resources, we'll never accomplish this goal.

Faced with the enormous task of building the temple, Solomon got wisdom. He gave his heart to seek and search out wisdom concerning all things. He didn't leave anything undone. Nothing in his life was out of balance. He didn't get wisdom for one part of his life and walk in ignorance in others. He used the wisdom of God to seek and search out all things.

Like Solomon, we, too, must become wise in the total balance of our lives. I can't be successful if my wife is unsuccessful. I can't be successful if my wife and I are successful, but my children are not. I can't be successful if my family is successful but your family is not. How is that success?

As the pastor and shepherd of my congregation, how can I be successful if my sheep are not successful? It's my job to lead them to success.

I can never count my success in the things I own, for things don't make me successful. My success and your success are found in the accomplishment of the vision and purpose that God has entrusted to us as individuals.

We have confused success with consumption. Often people will come to me and remark about how successful I am. I always tell them that I'm not successful—at least not yet. I'm on my way to success, and I'm much better off than I have been in the past. But I won't be successful until my church is filled with people who are prospering.

The Power to Get Wealth

We need to have enough wealth to influence the world for the gospel. We are called to influence people, to have enough power and influence to cause them to change the eternal destinies of their lives.

It will take money to touch the globe, and it will take a lot of it. You may be thinking, *Well, it's not about money.* I would like to show you in the Word of God where it tells us that it *is* about money—it's about a lot of money. If you read the book of Deuteronomy, you'll discover that these people had possessions. They owned houses and land and they had material possessions. In verse 8:18, you see where they became ignorant:

And thou say in thine heart, My power and the might of mine hand hath gotten me this wealth. But thou shalt remember the Lord thy God: for it is he that giveth thee power to get wealth, that he [God] may establish his covenant which he sware unto thy fathers, as it is this day.

—Deuteronomy 8:17-18

God said that He would give His people the power to get wealth. So if God didn't want you to have wealth, He wouldn't give you the power to get it.

Now when I read these verses, this is how I understand them: In Deuteronomy 8:18, God told His people that He would give us power to get wealth. This is not so that we can be wealthy, as if that were an end in itself. He gives us power to get wealth so that He can establish His covenant in the earth.

In other words, God says that it will take the power of wealth in order for His people to be able to establish His covenant.

The body of Christ is doing a pitiful job of establishing the covenant of God the way God intended, as it's written in the Bible. The problem is a problem of the heart. Do we as a people want to do what God said? People are ready and waiting to lay down their lives for the gospel, but they can't fulfill God's plans because they're broke. Don't ever say, "It's not about money."

You go to work every day because your employer promises you money. Whatever your salary is, it has had enough influence over your life to get you up every morning. Some people are in such bondage, not to wealth, but only to the money they get on their jobs, that they won't even let that go to obey God.

They think that because it's a secure job they cannot risk standing up for Jesus Christ in the workplace. I worked for the post office, which is considered a very secure job because it's a government job. A lot of people would kill for the security of a job at the post office. Such individuals must realize that a person can work for a company in America today and work hard every day, waiting to retire at forty-five years. When they get to the forty-forth year, they find the company is under new management that had decided to take a new direction. You find a pink slip in your mailbox telling you that you've got to go. You worked for forty-four years waiting on a broken promise.

You had better learn to place your trust in God and not your company. The Bible says, "Trust in the Lord with all thine heart; and lean not unto thine own understanding. In all thy ways acknowledge him, and he shall direct thy paths" (Prov. 3:5-6). Solomon's life was directed by the wisdom of God.

God told Solomon that because he asked for wisdom, God would give him riches and honor as well. Riches and honor follow wisdom. Therefore, if you don't have any money, it's possible that you also lack wisdom. You may have sown into ministries and have a great deal of seed in the ground. You may have a mighty anointing upon your life. You even may be called by God to do great things, but still you're broke. It could well be that what you're lacking is wisdom.

Conclusion

Perhaps God gave you wisdom at one point in your life, but you have not used it or applied it to your circumstances. You may have wisdom that you've never used—the very wisdom that will unlock the door to your success.

The book of Proverbs advises us, "Wisdom is the principal thing; therefore get wisdom: and with all thy getting get understanding" (Prov. 4:7). In all you do, in every dream and every goal in which you venture forth, know that wisdom will create a pathway to success. It is a pathway filled with abundant blessings that will take you into your wealthy place of godly inheritance.

Chapter 5

Gain Honor Through Wisdom

Solomon never killed a bear or a lion like his father David; he never faced a Goliath, fought in a battle or won a war. Yet Solomon was considered greater than his father because he had wisdom. Solomon's wisdom brought him great honor throughout the entire world, and wisdom can do the same for you.

When was the last time you had a challenge and sought God with all your heart to find out what you should do? That's what I do, and it has become a key to success for me. It will work the same way in your life as well.

Wealth, prosperity and much, much more will follow as you walk in wisdom. The Bible says that wisdom will bring you honor, too. Let's look.

> *And when the queen of Sheba heard of the fame of Solomon...*
>
> —1 Kings 10:1

How did Solomon get so famous? The last verses we read about him said he didn't know how to go out or how to come in. Here we see that his fame had spread throughout the world. What

happened during the time span between these two verses is that
he got wisdom. Solomon had been called to be king already. That
fact was established between God and his father, David.

Our forefathers fought a lot of battles, and they had to deal
with things that brought about blessings in which we can now
walk. Battles against racism and racial injustice were won by our
forefathers so that we can now walk in greater liberty than they
enjoyed. We don't need to deal with racism in the same ways our
fathers did, for that was then and this is now. Why would I use the
same methods used in the '60s to deal with racism in the 21st
century? We have an anointing in the 21st century to deal with it.
Therefore, we don't need to go backwards.

The Fame of Solomon

The queen of Sheba heard of the fame of Solomon and traveled
all the way to Israel to see if what she had heard about Solomon
was true. She came to test his great wisdom with hard questions.

And when the queen of Sheba heard of the fame of Solomon
concerning the name of the Lord, she came to prove him with
hard questions.

> *And she came to Jerusalem with a very great*
> *train, with camels that bare spices, and very*
> *much gold.*
>
> —1 Kings 10:1-2

We already saw that God said riches and honor would follow
wisdom. Now we see the queen of Sheba coming and bringing a

great amount of money with her. Isn't it interesting that Solomon didn't have to go out to get wealth. The wealth came to him as a result of his great wisdom.

> *And she came to Jerusalem with a very great train, with camels that bare spices, and very much gold, and precious stones: and when she was come to Solomon, she communed with him of all that was in her heart. And Solomon told her all her questions: there was not any thing hid from the king, which he told her not. And when the queen of Sheba had seen...*
>
> —1 Kings 10:2-4

The queen heard of him and she came a long way to see his possessions — she wanted to see his stuff. When the lady showed up, she saw before she ever heard anything. If she would have arrived and seen Solomon living in some little, old shack beside the road, she would not have been impressed. She would have thought that someone had lied to her about his greatness. She would not have given him all of the gold she brought with her.

That's why I look a certain way. If you look as if you ought to have money, when the money shows up, it says, "This is my home. That looks like a place where I belong."

Recently, many people celebrated Black History Month, and an announcement was made that a new housing project was being named after someone who had been active in civil rights. What kind of an honor is it to have a housing project named after you? That's no honor.

It was announced that a certain housing project would be torn down and a new one built within five years. When I heard it I became indignant. Understand that the underlying assumption regarding the people who live in the project is that their circumstances would never change. Five years from now the city was making plans for their children's children to live in the same housing projects.

Some people actually received the news with a sense of celebration. Something is seriously wrong when we sit back and say this kind of thing is acceptable.

It doesn't matter where a person started in life, for everyone has to start somewhere. The Bible says, "Though thy beginning was small, yet thy latter end should greatly increase" (Job 8:7). Where you were when you started out in life is not even an issue. What's important is where you are headed. What is your desire? What is inside of you?

Don't ever accept such low expectations. For it's a well-known fact that each of us will rise to the level of our expectations. If you expect to live and die in a housing project, you probably will. But if you expect to be full of wisdom and have success and wealth follow you, your life will rise to the level of those expectations.

I know some people think that these projects were old, and it would be a great improvement to have new ones built. But these people don't understand the underlying message of defeat. How much better would it be if there were nobody poor enough to live in government funded housing in five years? How much better would it be to fund a plan and some programs to help people get so far removed from poverty that there won't be anyone needing such housing?

It's for reasons such as these that God is giving us wisdom to bring in great wealth so that this cycle of low expectations and poverty can be brought to an end. This wisdom produces something visible in the material realm. Let's look:

> *And when the queen of Sheba had seen all Solomon's wisdom...*
>
> —1 Kings 10:4

When the queen of Sheba saw Solomon's wealth, the Bible suggests that she saw his wisdom. The fruit of Solomon's wisdom was all that he built. His wisdom produced something in the material realm.

In my life, wisdom has produced a jet. The reason why we own a jet is because of the wisdom that I've received from God. I believe that every time we land our jet God is honored. When we land our jet we are displaying the fulfillment of the vision of God in this ministry. Hundreds of jets take off every day that are not serving God's purposes on earth, but ours is helping to fulfill our calling to preach the gospel.

Some people are shocked when they see the ministry's jet. They feel that we're just too prosperous. But it's God's intention to cause His people to prosper greatly.

Now, look:

> *And when the queen of Sheba had seen all*
> *Solomon's wisdom, and the house that he had*
> *built, And the meat of his table, and the sitting*
> *of his servants, and the attendance of his*
> *ministers, and their apparel, and his*
> *cupbearers, and his ...*
>
> —1 Kings 10:4-5

You can bet that Solomon wasn't eating Spam or Kentucky Fried Chicken or Hamburger Helper without the hamburger. The queen of Sheba was overwhelmed at the incredible prosperity that she encountered when she visited Solomon. Not only was Solomon prosperous, but everyone around him was also extremely prosperous. Everywhere she looked the queen saw wealth, but she called it Solomon's wisdom.

Walking with Wisdom

Even the way Solomon carried himself spoke of the wealth brought about by his wisdom. Solomon had built an entrance for himself into the temple that impressed the queen of Sheba.

> *...and his ascent by which he went up into the*
> *house of the Lord.*
>
> —1 Kings 10:5

It's interesting that Solomon in his great wisdom felt that it was important to come to the house of worship in a certain way. Wisdom says that you don't come to church any kind of way. I'm not necessarily talking about what you wear. Never feel that if you don't own a suit you cannot come to church. I'm talking about the way you walk, your countenance, the way you carry yourself or what your face looks like.

People with wisdom walk a certain way. Wealthy people walk a certain way, and they look a certain way.

My son tells me that I walk like I own stuff. Wherever you go, man, walk like you own the place. When I go to Charleston I walk like I own Charleston.

Don't go to the bank like you're sneaking around. If you do, the managers might suspect that you're trying to rob it. Instead, get your shoulders up and walk into the bank as if you belong in a bank.

The Report Was True

The queen of Sheba had come a long way to find out for herself if Solomon was as wise and great as she had heard. Here's what she had to say about all that she'd heard.

> *And she said to the king, It was a true report that I heard in mine own land of thy acts and of thy wisdom.*
>
> —1 Kings 10:6

This passage provides some insight into why our soul winning efforts have been unsuccessful. People hear about us Christians and come to see if what they hear is true. But when they show up, we have to be able to show them the evidence of what we've spoken to them about. If we tell them that the wisdom of God has produced blessings in our lives, we must be able to show them the results. Solomon was certainly able to do that.

Now, every one of us is at a different level of growth and maturity. Solomon told us in the book of Ecclesiastes that he had to go and search out and seek out all things. So everything didn't just magically, instantly appear for him. He had to undergo a process to get to where he was. And that's what this book is teaching you to do as well.

Let's take a look at what the queen of Sheba said about Solomon.

> *And she said to the king, It was a true report that I heard in mine own land of thy acts and of thy wisdom. Howbeit I believed not the words, until I came, and mine eyes had seen it: and, behold, the half was not told me: thy wisdom and prosperity exceedeth the fame which I heard. Happy are thy men, happy are these thy servants, which stand continually before thee, and that hear thy wisdom.*
>
> —1 Kings 10:6-8

Wisdom also makes you happy. When you're constantly standing before a man of God with wisdom, then you're going to be happy. If you're not, something is wrong with you. I'm happy. My life is good, and it's getting better every day.

My wife and I have applied these teachings for years. We read the Word of God, believe it and act on it, expecting God to fulfill His promises. We refuse to doubt the Word of God.

In everything that God has told me to do, I approach with His wisdom. Good ideas will not produce the wealth that God is talking about through these scriptures. We need God ideas. We must be led by, influenced by and directed by the wisdom of God, just like Solomon.

Building the Truth Dome

We are planning to build a 15,000-seat dome for a ministry in Tampa Bay, Florida called the Truth Dome. God has placed this project on my heart. To begin building this dream, I started with wisdom. I began seeking and searching out everything concerning the Truth Dome. We had to determine how much land we would need and where it should be located. Such a structure needs to be built in the right place. If you purchase land in the wrong place — for instance, where there are no utilities coming up to it such as sewage, water and power — then you will end up paying a lot more money to help create an infrastructure. So we had to learn about the infrastructure. We had to investigate the roads. What kind of access would such a project require? That's the information and the wisdom we had to seek and search out.

Before we purchased the land, we paid engineers to go in and find out if we could build on that land. What if we bought the land and found out later that we couldn't build on it? Then we would have paid all that money for land we couldn't build on. No, we're smarter than that, because we have the wisdom of God.

If you make all of your decisions based upon God's wisdom, you will succeed every time. You will never fail and you will never start something you cannot finish. What would happen if every decision concerning your family were based on the wisdom of God? You'd be successful 100 percent of the time!

Wealth and Wisdom

Let's look at the final scriptures in this passage.

> *And she gave the king an hundred and twenty talents of gold, and of spices very great store, and precious stones: there came no more such abundance of spices as these which the queen of Sheba gave to king Solomon. And the navy also of Hiram, that brought gold from Ophir, brought in from Ophir great plenty of almug trees, and precious stones.*
>
> —1 Kings 10:10-11

In reading this, are you asking yourself, *Wasn't he already rich?* Didn't God tell Solomon that when he got wisdom, wealth and honor would follow? When wealth gets into the hands of a man or woman with wisdom, others will prosper, too.

Because of the wisdom of God, this ministry—this one single church—has caused increase in businesses. At least one contracting company has greatly increased in wealth.

What do you think is going to happen when we continue to the next phase of our building project? Other companies that will be working with us on the project will be increased, also.

It all began with the wisdom of God. Because of God's wisdom there are forty-nine people employed by this ministry. Forty-nine people are not on welfare and are contributing to the financial well-being of this community. We employ everyone from teachers with master's degrees to aircraft pilots because of the wisdom of God.

How much bigger can it get? There are no limits. The school at the Truth Dome site will house 300 students. How many teachers is that? It won't be long before universities and colleges will be sending recruiters to us to try to get some teachers in here. We'll be a resource center for them.

The sound system in the Truth Dome will cost about $1.4 million. Those kinds of costs could start a company.

The queen of Sheba came with great wealth, but watch what Solomon does with the wealth that she placed in his hands. This is what happens when you place wealth into the hands of a wise person and not a fool.

And the king made of the almug trees pillars for the house of the Lord. . .And king Solomon gave unto the queen of Sheba all her desire, whatsoever she asked, besides that which Solomon gave her of his royal bounty. So she

*turned and went to her own country, she and
her servants.*

—1 Kings 10:12-13

If you continue reading this passage, it tells you just how much wealth came to Solomon every year. Why? It all started with wisdom.

Conclusion

Don't let anyone talk you out of the wealth that God has called you to reap and harvest. He has done so in order for you to see the fulfillment of His vision in your life. Others may tell you that it's God's will for you to be poor. But they're just wrong. God desires you to be rich—rich in honor, wisdom and blessings—rich enough to accomplish the great vision that He has for you on this earth. If you will seek God for His wisdom, He will provide unlimited wealth through you in order to enable you to finance your part of the spreading of the gospel.

Chapter 6

Cultivate Godly Self-Confidence

There is no reason that you cannot experience total success in your life. The time of canceling out God's blessings in your life is behind you. The fifth vital key to experiencing that success is succeeding at being you. You need to learn how to be the best you that you can possibly be by cultivating godly self-confidence.

Nobody can be you better than you, for there's not anyone or anything else on earth like you. You are uniquely you. God made you. He created you. You're not an accident. Scientifically, you're one in a million. And I believe you're one in a million whose gifts can produce at least a million dollars.

The book of 2 Samuel contains some valuable keys to learning how to succeed at being you. Let's take a look.

Now when Mephibosheth, the son of Jonathan, the son of Saul, was come unto David, he fell on his face, and did reverence. And David said, Mephibosheth. And he answered, Behold thy servant!

And David said unto him, Fear not: for I will surely show thee kindness for Jonathan thy father's sake, and will restore thee all the land of Saul thy father; and thou shalt eat bread at my table continually.

—2 Samuel 9:6-7

It's important to understand why David said this. David was a warrior king, and it was expected that after a new king ascended to the throne the members of the former king's family would be seen as enemies and would be killed. Therefore, Mephibosheth, who was the former king Saul's grandson, feared that David wanted to kill him. But David didn't intend to kill him at all.

Life was about to get much better for Mephibosheth because of the king's favor, just as things are getting better for you. Your finances are getting better; your marriage is getting better; your relationship with your family is getting better; your relationship with God is getting better — everything is getting better for you because of God's favor in your life. This year will be your best year yet, and your life is getting better every day.

Everything was about to get better for Mephibosheth because of the covenant his father Jonathan made with David. But look at Mephibosheth's response.

And he bowed himself, and said, What is thy servant, that thou shouldest look upon such a dead dog as I am?

—2 Samuel 9:8

Talk about low self-esteem! This man called himself a dead dog. Low self-esteem is a major hindrance to walking in the success to which God has called us. Therefore, we must deal with it by learning to develop a godly self-esteem.

Are you at the same place that Mephibosheth found himself? Is God saying one thing about you, but you are unable to receive it? Are you responding much like Mephibosheth responded to David by telling God that you're not worthy to receive His blessings? Do you say, "Well some folks can receive success and prosperity, but not me."

Why not you? If your self-esteem is so low that you cannot receive God's blessings in your life, let's get into God's Word together so that with His help, you can begin walking in a new level of godly self-esteem.

You ought to be feeling good about yourself every day. Even if you don't feel good about what's going on around you, you still ought to feel good about yourself. Feeling good about yourself has nothing to do with how your physical body may be reacting to whatever is going on around you on a particular day. Your body is little more than a suit made of flesh, blood and bones. But it is just your suit, and your suit is not what makes you feel good or bad. The real you is on the inside of that suit.

You are different from everybody else walking the planet. You are a completely unique act of God's creative genius, a powerful part of His creative plan for this earth.

If we don't understand that there is something very special about us and that we have to love ourselves, then we're going to allow others to abuse us. We're going to allow others to take advantage of us because we don't think much of ourselves.

Managing Relationships

How you think about yourself will affect everything in your entire life, including your success at business. Business is about relationships. A successful businessman knows how to manage the relationships that are necessary for the success of his business. What makes that man successful is how he manages the relationships.

How you manage your relationship as a husband or wife will determine whether your marriage will succeed. How you handle or view your relationship with God will ultimately determine two very important things—your relationship with yourself and your relationship with others.

In the world, people make decisions or determinations about a person's ability to be successful based upon their own perceptions, not on God's. The world believes that if you are obese, you cannot be successful. If you're too thin, you cannot be successful. If you're too tall or too short, your success will be impaired. If you're too this or too that, if you're too black, too white, too yellow, too purple, whatever. This kind of thinking is completely unbiblical and totally wrong.

We've got to find greater wisdom than what's been presented to us by the world to help us create healthy relationships that will cause us to love ourselves as God loves us.

If you've got a business selling anything, if you don't love yourself, then you're not going to love your customers. If you want them to buy your product but you don't really care that much about them, then you're not going to be very successful selling your product. Proverbs 23:7 says,

For as he thinketh in his heart, so is he.

We can say it like this: "As a man thinketh in his heart, so is he." The way you think about yourself, the way you view yourself and what you see when you look at yourself in the mirror are going to have a great deal to do with what you project to others. And what you project to others will determine how they view you.

Overcoming Self-Rejection

You are responsible for what image you're projecting. And you cannot project the image of yourself properly if you don't love yourself.

Self-rejection and even self-hatred are root causes of many relationship problems. How can a man love his wife if he doesn't love himself? How can a woman love her husband if she doesn't love herself? And how can you love your children if you don't love yourself?

The Word of God also links self-love with our ability to love others when it says, "Thou shalt love thy neighbor as thyself" (Matt. 19:19). In other words, your ability to love another individual will be limited by your ability to love and accept yourself.

How can someone who is filled with self-rejection and self-hatred succeed at anything? Every time that individual looks at herself, she sees something wrong. You can never get away from you! You'll be right here with yourself until Jesus comes.

You may have to work with some people you don't like. You love your job, but you hate to go to work on some days because you're forced to be around certain people. But no matter how difficult some people are at work, you still get to go home and be away from them for several hours, knowing that you won't have to deal with them until it's time to go back to work. But you can't leave you.

Now, a lot of people try to leave themselves through drugs and other avenues of escape. But sooner or later they discover that it doesn't work. When they come back down they still must deal with themselves.

Some people have been convinced by other people that they're ugly. Therefore, because they feel they're ugly—because that's what they've been told all their lives—they reject themselves to the point at which they start to hate themselves.

Others are blessed with great physical beauty, yet they still hate themselves. They can only see what is wrong with themselves. Someone along the way planted seeds of self-hatred and self-rejection into them. If that sounds like you, then you're never going to get to the place where God wants you to be until you deal with that self-rejection. You're going to always be looking at other people and measuring yourself by them.

I could line up twenty people and every one of them would be different. In a room of thousands, each person in that room is completely unique. And no one is ugly, unless he or she accepts someone's particular definition of what ugly is.

I planted that seed of self-acceptance in my children. I tell them often that they are good looking because they look like themselves. They are the best looking them that exists!

The Bible teaches us that we must have a deep love for others. Let's look:

> *Finally, all [of you] should be of one and the same mind (united in spirit), sympathizing [with one another], loving [each other] as brethren [of one household], compassionate and courteous (tender-hearted and humble).*
>
> —1 Peter 3:8, (AMP)

Don't ever put another person down. That individual is better at being himself or herself than anyone else. He is better at being himself than you are at being him. I'm always better than you at being me. You ought to be better than me at being you, even though I'm not trying to be you. You are the best!

The Bible says,

> *But on the contrary blessing [praying for their welfare, happiness, and protection, and truly pitying and loving them]. For know that to this you have been called, that you may yourselves inherit a blessing [from God – that you may obtain a blessing as heirs, bringing welfare and happiness and protection].*
>
> *For let him who wants to enjoy life and see good days [good – whether apparent or not] keep his tongue free from evil and his lips from guile (treachery, deceit). Let him turn away from wickedness and shun it, and let him do right. Let him search for peace (harmony; undisturbedness from fears, agitating passions, and moral conflicts) and seek it eagerly. [Do not merely desire peaceful relations with God, with your fellowmen, and {with who?} yourself, but pursue, go after them!*

—1 Peter 3:9-11(AMP)

This passage says that if we want to be blessed, we need to stay away from deceit. But we haven't done that. Somebody lied to us and told us there was something wrong with loving ourselves and feeling good about ourselves, and we believed it.

You may think that seems arrogant. However, if you wait for other people to tell you what to think about yourself, you'll be up one day and down the next. People will love you today and hate you tomorrow. That's what happened to Jesus. One day they were waving palm branches at Him, praising Him as the Messiah, and a few days later the same people were crying, "Crucify Him!"

Loving Yourself and Loving Others

Do not merely desire a peaceful relationship with God. It doesn't stop there. You may tell yourself that you love God. But you really can't completely love God and hate yourself, because He lives inside of you. The reason He moved into your life is so that you would know love and know how to love Him.

So if you don't know love, you can't love Him. If you don't love Him, you don't love yourself. And if you don't love yourself, you don't love your fellowman. And God said if you don't love your fellowman, how can you say you love me? (See 1 John 4:20).

We sit around not loving ourselves, even though God has said some great things about us. Do not merely desire peaceful relations with God, with your fellowman and with yourself. Pursue a peaceful relationship with God. Pursue a peaceful relationship with your fellowman. Pursue a peaceful relationship with yourself. Go after it.

Who You Are In Christ

What kind of relationship should we have with God, with ourselves and, ultimately, with our fellowman? Romans 5 tells us. It says,

> *And hope maketh not ashamed; because the love of God is shed abroad in our hearts by the Holy Ghost which is given unto us.For when we were yet without strength, in due time, [or in the due season, in the process of time, at the right time] Christ [the Anointed One] died for the ungodly. For scarcely for a righteous man will one die: yet, peradventure for a good man some would even dare to die.*
>
> *But God commendeth his love toward us, in that, while we were yet sinners...*
>
> —Romans 5:5-8

What? God loved you when you were a low-down, dirty dog; untrustworthy, lying, thieving, whoremongering, drunken, dope smoking, pill popping, partying hardy all night long, waking up in the bed with somebody you didn't know, sinner. While we were living in sin, God was saying, "I love you."

He loved you enough that he commended His love toward you in that, while you were yet a sinner, Christ, the Anointed One, died for you. Much more then, being now justified by His blood, you shall be saved from wrath through Him.

We frequently try to deal with the bad fruit in our lives. A lot of us have bad fruit. As a matter of fact, everyone has a little bad fruit. Some have more of it, and some have truckloads of bad fruit. We all have some things we need to get straightened out. We all have some problems, some challenges, some areas in our lives where the love of God keeps us until God can perfect us.

If this were not true in your life, you would be like Enoch, you would have been translated already.

Getting to the Root of Your Bad Fruit

We frequently attempt to deal with the bad fruit in our lives and never get to the root cause of that bad fruit. Some people try to stop getting drunk, but they never deal with what is causing them to drink. Why would you go get so drunk you can't even see straight?

Before I was saved, I did a lot of drinking. I remember one time I went to a party, and it was raining and kind of muddy everywhere. I got out of the car and stepped right in mud. This was in Alabama where we had a kind of red mud, so it was a mess.

I was walking towards this entrance to the party, and before you got to the sidewalk that led into the place, there was a wire down near the ground to keep cars from driving beyond the parking lot into the grass. Well, I didn't see the wire. There was no sign posted to warn us in the dark that the wire was there. So I tripped over the wire and fell right in the mud.

What did I do? I was so drunk that I got up and went on in the party, mud and everything. I didn't know. I don't call it alcohol. I call it ignorant oil. That's what that ignorant oil will do to you. I'm there at the party thinking I'm cool — I'm making it happen — and I've got mud all over my pants and shirt.

On another occasion as a young man, I was driving my motorcycle, and I loved to drive fast. I felt that if a speedometer was marked to go as high as 150 mph, then I should drive that fast. There were times when I would try to do that 150 mph as I traveled from one club to the next.

One particular road that I loved to ride on had s-curves. And I would get on my bike at 1 or 2 a.m. after I'd been drinking from 5 or 6 p.m. One club would be closing, and I would have to get to an after-hours club.

One night on my way to this after-hours club, I approached the s-curve, and I had this false sense that the drunker I got the better I thought I could drive. That's what that ignorant oil will do to you. It will make you think you're Mario Andretti.

So there I went, zooming down the road headed for that s-curve. I came through the first curve fine. I used to love to hang down on the bike until the metal dragged on the ground, spitting little sparks from the kickstand.

On the next curve, I literally had to shift all my bodyweight over to rebalance the bike to make the next curve. Well, when you're drunk things don't work properly. I waited too long to re-shift my bodyweight and caught that curve. The bike flipped.

Drunks often walk away from their car accidents, which was what I did. But my beautiful motorcycle had a big dent in the tank. That Yamaha was metallic black with metallic flakes in it, and it was beautiful.

When I got it back up, the carburetors were flooded, and the handle bar was bent up. I drained all the gas out of the carburetor and started it back up. Did I go home? No. I went on to the club with blood all over my jacket.

It wasn't until about 8 A.M. the next morning when I got home that I really realized what had taken place. After I parked the motorcycle in their garage, I sat down on my momma and daddy's step and cried. I was saying, *My bike, my bike.* I was just sitting there going through this, and Daddy came out there and put his hands on me and said, "That's all right. We can get another motorcycle, but you're all right."

I went from thinking that I was literally invincible and could not die to the point where I didn't really like to live. But I had no intention of committing suicide. I figured that if you committed suicide then you would go to hell. Now, I wasn't saved, so I was on my way to hell already, but this is still how I thought.

Getting In Touch with the Roots of My Bad Fruit

Why was I drinking and living so recklessly? There were issues in my life that I hadn't dealt with. There were things I didn't understand about life itself. I didn't know life, and I didn't know love.

I didn't really believe in everybody's concept of love, and much of that attitude was rooted in the fact that I had been adopted. My mother was about 15 years old when I was born, and I just didn't think anybody loved me. I always thought that somebody was running a game or running a scam. Therefore, I trusted very few people.

There were only two people whom I trusted. One of them was my wife, Deborah, and one of them was an uncle. I didn't even trust my own mother and father, my adoptive parents who raised me, until I got saved.

I had issues in my life, and I didn't understand myself. I didn't really like "me" very much. Now people were always telling me how successful I would be at one thing or another. I was an artist, and I could paint and sculpt. But when people tried to encourage me in my gifts, I would just go get drunk.

Losing Oneself

The worst thing that I ever did was to start partying and getting drunk, because you can really lose yourself around other phony people. The night club scene is comprised of phony people. You listen to whoever tells the biggest lie, those who can make others believe that lie they're selling. I fell into that lifestyle for a long time and actually enjoyed it.

I used to play little roles with people, which required that I create a new identity, another me. I worked as a record promoter, and whatever I needed to do and be at the moment, that's what I would do and the role I would play. I drove myself to do this by drinking alcohol, so people thought I had a drinking problem. Really, I didn't have a drinking problem as much as I had a lack of self-love problem. I didn't love me. That low self-image impacted every other area of my life.

I didn't really love my wife, Deborah, in the way that God calls men to love their wives. But I didn't realize that at the time. All I knew was that I needed someone stable in my life. She was stable, but I wasn't faithful to her, and it wasn't something that mattered to me at the time. I really didn't even want to get married when we did, but I did so because she refused to shack up.

I weighed the situation and said, *Well, what's the difference? I'm going to sleep around anyway, so if she wants to get married then I'll marry her and still sleep around*, which is what I did. I slept with someone else on the day before our wedding, and I had no guilt about it.

I didn't understand that if you love someone then there are things you don't do. I couldn't conceive that.

When we had our son Greg, I didn't really love him either. There were times that I'd get really angry with him, like when we had very little money to buy food. Once we had some corn flakes and just a little milk. So, I drank the milk and poured water on his corn flakes. I reasoned that he was just a baby, so what did he know? What would be the difference? When people don't know how to love that's the way they live.

Seeing the Root

I needed to deal with the root of my problem. The root involved how I felt about myself, for how you treat others is really a reflection of how you feel about yourself. If you cheat yourself, you don't have a problem cheating others. And you cheat yourself every time you don't obey the Word of God. Every time you don't do what the Word of God says to do but do what you want to do, you're cheating yourself.

If you will do that to yourself, there's no limit to what you will do to others, except for the limits placed upon you by your fears. The only thing that kept me from certain activities was the fear of jail. Whenever I thought about doing something illegal, I always had the thought, *but what if you get caught?*

As much as I love now, I hated then. Back then I couldn't care less about people. I had zero tolerance for people I didn't really like. Most people were nonexistent as far as I was concerned. That was hatred, which I had because I didn't know how to love.

The Bible says this about love:

> *For the whole Law [concerning human relationships] is compiled within one precept: You shall love your neighbor as [you do] yourself.*
> —Galatians 5:14 (AMP)

The whole law concerning human relationships is compiled within the one precept: Love your neighbor as you love yourself.

Perfecting Love Within Us

It is possible to really change in Christ. I love people now—If they only knew how much I love them! Now I have the love of God, and I don't love you based on what you do or don't do. I love you because God loves me and I love Him. But if I say that I love Him, and I don't love you like I love Him, then I don't really love Him.

Look at 1 John 4:15-16,18:

> *Whosoever shall confess that Jesus is the son of God, God dwelleth in him, and he in God.*

And we have known and believed the love that God hath to us. God is love; and he that dwelleth in love dwelleth in God, and God in him...There is no fear in love; but perfect love casteth out fear.

Why is it so hard for us to accept what God is saying about His love towards us? Because we don't love ourselves. See, if you don't love yourself the way God loves you then it's difficult for you to conceive anybody loving you, especially God. So what will happen is you will reject every attempt that God makes to bring you back to where you need to be. You keep rejecting Him. God says, "Come on."

You say, "I'm not worthy."

God says, "Come on. It'll be all right. Come on."

"No, not this time. I've messed up too bad."

God says, "I'm waiting on you. I'm tired of the devil using you. I love you. He hates you. Come on."

"I can't do it. God, your love is too much for me." And you turn around and walk away.

One of the most difficult things in marriage is trying to prove to your spouse that you love him or her when that person does not love himself or herself. That's why a lot of relationships have problems. You can say and do all you can to affirm her and encourage her in your love. But if your wife doesn't love herself, then she will not be able to rest in your love for her.

Self-Acceptance and Change

Rejecting ourselves does not change us. Instead, it actually increases our problems. But when you accept yourself, you accept everything about yourself. That means you've got to deal with yourself, now. You've got to deal with what's wrong with you. You cannot do that until you first accept yourself. We need to agree with God that when He created us, He created something good.

If you read in the book of Genesis where God created man, He said that His creation was good. As a matter of fact, the Amplified Version says you were approved and accepted.

Amos 3:3 says, _"Can two walk together, except they be agreed?"_ Well, God is saying one thing, but when you reject yourself you're saying something different.

Change requires correction. When you change, you don't do the same thing and just say, "I'm changing." You must make corrections to what you're doing wrong. Golfers are always coming across the green to show one another what they are doing wrong and how they need to make corrections. That's what we need to do with ourselves in order to improve.

But you've got to be willing to change. If you don't make the corrections, then you're not going to see yourself the way God sees you, which means you're not in agreement with Him. If you're not in agreement with God, He's not walking with you. He's just standing there waiting on you. While you're going the wrong way, He's waiting on you to notice that you've gone the wrong way, you've developed the wrong attitude and you are seeing yourself the wrong way. He's waiting on you to change. He is just standing right there where you left Him. He's just waiting on you to notice that what you're doing isn't working.

When we finally notice how we're wrong, we want to sit down in the mess and say, "Lord, please come get me out of this."

He'll say, "No, you walked over there. You get up and walk on back over here to me. Come on back."

Self-Love and Correction

People who do not know they are loved have a very difficult time receiving correction. If you're a parent, then this could be a problem when you try to correct your children. The problem wasn't that they didn't want to be corrected, but that's what you assumed.

The problem was that you didn't show them enough love for them to receive your correction.

You can't just beat somebody up, correcting them all the time. Every now and then you've got to say, "Hey, that's good. I'm so proud of you."

Many of you are wounded today because all you heard all of your life was criticism. Your parents didn't know any better. They probably received the same thing as they were growing up. This is especially true for men. Our society doesn't give men permission to have problems. They're supposed to always be strong.

Jesus is your help. But you won't accept Him as your helper until you first admit that you need help. Likewise, people who do not know they are loved have a very difficult time receiving correction.

I can spend a lot of time correcting someone, but my time is wasted unless that individual receives what I've said. Don't ever spend your time trying to correct somebody with whom you haven't first built a relationship, because you're wasting your time. You can only correct people with whom you've built a relationship—people who feel that you care about them.

If you tell me that I'm wrong, it won't help me unless you also tell me how to make it right. I'll receive it if I believe that you care about me.

Steps to Developing Godly Self-Confidence

Here are seven steps that if followed will help you develop godly self-confidence.

1. Recognize that God wants good things for you (See James 1:17).

2. Make certain that your dream is not contrary to the laws of God or man.

3. Fill every conversation with faith-talk about your dream.

4. Associate often with those whose fire is presently burning brighter than your own.

5. Remember that your own dream is a special seed you are sowing into the hearts of others.

6. Remember that your dream may intimidate those close to you and make them feel uncomfortable.

7. Don't force your dreams on others.

Conclusion

Love and godly self-confidence are mighty keys to the growth and change that will ultimately open the doors of success to you and to those around you. As you continue to learn self-acceptance and self-love, always know that you are walking in agreement with a God who loved you so much that He died for you on a cross. He created you to be one of a kind, and nobody can be a better you than you! You're one in a million!

Chapter 7

Expect and Prepare for Your Future Success

Your success will require a great deal of determination. The next vital success principle we will explore involves your expectations and preparations for future success. Your future in God is very bright. Therefore, be determined that you will not live below the level of blessings that God has prepared for your future.

Now when you determine something, you make a bold, unwavering decision. You set your mind and your affections on accomplishing what you've decided to do. When you fail to make a decision, you leave your future and your destiny up to chance. You know the saying, "whatever will be will be." This attitude is a formula for failure.

God wants you successful in every area of your life. True prosperity is not limited to increasing financial blessings in your life. If you are a mean spirited person, money won't change your disposition. If you are ill, money can't make you well. If no one likes you because of your bad attitude, then money won't change your attitude. Prosperity includes blessings in every area of need.

It's getting better for you. Your marriage, your finances, your health, your job, your business — everything is getting better. Jeremiah 29:11 says,

> *For I know the thoughts that I think toward you, saith the Lord, thoughts of peace, and not of evil.*

God Is Thinking About You

Whether or not you are aware of it, God is thinking about you. While you're putting yourself down, God is thinking good thoughts about you. While you're letting your past determine your future, God is planning better things for you. While you're looking at all the opportunities that you've already missed, God is at work creating even better ones for you. He says that His thoughts about you are for peace. He says that He plans for you to lack nothing--to have nothing within you that's broken. He said His thoughts are of peace and not of evil.

God is not looking for things to turn out badly for you. Even if you say, *Yeah, but God doesn't know what I did.*

God knows exactly what you've done. You must understand that you are not God and God is not you. Thank God for that! When you are ready to give up because everything around you appears bad, that's when God says, "Now that you can't make it happen, it's finally time for you to just shut down and let Me take over."

When you finally run out of you, that's when you're in the best position you've ever been to see the manifestation of God's power. When you get to the end of self then He can take over, because you are no longer trying to fix it. You've finally learned that you can never fix it.

God said that He knows the thoughts that He has toward you. But do *you* know His thoughts toward you? If you get a thought that comes to you and it is not good, then it has not come from God. Do you have thoughts about how worthless and unlovable you are? Such thoughts are not from God, because He says that His thoughts toward you are good and not evil.

Satan is also in the spirit realm, and he's a fallen angel. Sometimes he can deceive you by giving you the impression that he's God, and then he can fill your mind with destructive thoughts.

Often, godly people can behave in foolish ways because they neglect to search out the Scriptures to make sure that what they are hearing is from God. God wrote the entire Bible, and He gave it to us to help us to know the truth in every situation.

The sons and daughters of God are led by the Spirit of God. Therefore, we are constructed by God to be led by spiritual things. Nevertheless, demons are also spirits, and the devil himself is a spirit being who lives in the realm of the spirit. Therefore, it's vitally important that, when you hear something from the spiritual realm, you discern whether or not it comes from God.

That's one reason that God gives us His peace. The Bible says we are to be led by peace (see Phil. 4:7).

Have you ever started to make a purchase and had no peace about spending the money? It just didn't feel like the right thing to do. It was probably the Spirit of God telling you not to buy that item right then. Have you ever had someone approach you, and, without saying a word, something about that person made you feel uncomfortable? You just didn't have any peace about that particular individual. The Holy Ghost inside of you was telling you something about that person.

Now, it's important to be aware of the fact that God is not double minded. If you hear a voice or have an impression that comes from the realm of the Spirit, and it doesn't line up with the Word of God, then it wasn't from God. His written Word will always agree with His spoken word. The Word and the Spirit will always agree.

God's objective in your life is to do you good and to make you happy because of His great, unconditional love for you. Unconditional love is not based upon any deeds that you have done or left undone. Neither is it based on how holy you are. Unconditional love is based entirely upon His great love towards you.

Have you been feeling a little down or feeling a little worthless and guilty lately? If so, I'm going to give you a scripture that will bless you and set you free forever. It's found in the book of Romans:

There is therefore now no condemnation to them which are in Christ Jesus, who walk not after the flesh, but after the Spirit.

—Romans 8:1

For I know the thoughts that I think toward you, saith the Lord, thoughts of peace and not of evil to give you an expected end.

—Jeremiah 29:11

Most people are fearful about tomorrow because they don't know what's going to happen. Most people are fearful of getting involved in relationships because they don't know if those relationships will be good or bad. They wonder, *is that person going to hurt me or love me? Is this going to be good or bad?*

But God doesn't treat you like that. God assures you that you never need to wonder how your relationship with Him will turn out. You needn't even concern yourself with the future because He knows what the future will be like.

Are you married? When you got married you had great expectations regarding your marriage, didn't you? On the day you were married, your expectation was that it would be good. The only things that may have later changed that expectation were your circumstances.

God Is Above Your Circumstances

God says that He is above situations and circumstances. Therefore, even if negative events and circumstances come into your life, He will make them turn out for your good if you keep your eyes on Him. Numbers 23:19 says, "God is not a man, that he should lie; neither the son of man, that he should repent."

If God said it, then He will do it, for He's made a commitment to Himself that He would bring it to pass. If I say that I'm going to become successful, but that success is based upon my own power and strength, then the outcome will be subject to a lot of factors such as getting the right breaks and circumstances. But if God says I'm going to be successful, that's an entirely different story. Well, God said that you were going to be successful. In fact, He calls you a success and not a failure.

> *For I know the thoughts that I think toward you, saith the Lord, thoughts of peace, and not of evil, to give you an expected end. Then shall ye call upon me, and ye shall go and pray unto me, and I will hearken unto you. And ye shall seek me, and find me, when ye shall search for me with all your heart.*
>
> —Jeremiah 29:11-13

Your part in your own success is to keep seeking God. Offer God what you have; this is what you do when you are saved. Then God gives us what He has, which really means that He's not getting the better part of the deal. God's love for us is what makes it a good deal for Him.

He takes all of our sins, faults, weaknesses and failures, and He gives us His righteousness and strength. He takes our poverty and gives us His wealth. He takes our diseases and sicknesses and gives us His healing and health. He takes our messed up, broken down lives and exchanges them for a hopeful, bright future.

One of the best things about this exchange is that God is always consistent. It doesn't matter how many times you fall down, when you get back up God still has a bright future for you. It doesn't matter how many times you miss it, how many times you mess up, when you get back to God you'll find that He hasn't moved and He hasn't changed.

Why Do We Fail?

Why, then, do we fail? When we take our own positions instead of God's, then we falter and fail. That's because so often we choose to feel sorry for ourselves or we want others to feel sorry for us so that we can remain lazy. God's pathway for us will not allow that.

Take A Hold of Your Success

Now that you know success is assured to you in God you must lay hold of it. One powerful step in laying hold of your future involves focusing on where you are headed. To be successful you must shake off your past and set your sights on the future.

God shared something with me years ago, and I've confessed it over and over and over again until it's become a part of my everyday walk. Satan will always take something from your past to use as evidence against you in the present to keep you from your future. Every time you've become discouraged or depressed, it was usually over something that Satan took from your past to get you depressed in the present, which caused you to lose focus of your future. As a result, you stopped expecting things to get better and shifted into a survival mode. When you begin to merely survive it means that you are not longer preparing for your future.

Therefore, when you finally arrive at your future you find that nothing is there because you didn't prepare for it. You lost your expectations for your future. You might even find that you've taken the wrong road and missed your future entirely.

God's Looking Out for You

God is looking out for you because He has good plans for you. Everything is going to be better. As a matter of fact, it's getting better right now. Angels are working on your behalf, working out your situation. You're going to make it.

The other day on the radio a man was criticizing ministries that teach that good is coming to God's people. He said that we are deceived for believing that God is taking us to a wealthy, prosperous place and that things are getting better. This radio teacher declared that everything is going to get much worse.

However, if you reject prosperity what do you have left? All that's left for you to believe in is gloom and doom.

Later in the broadcast he told his listeners that he didn't have enough money to stay on the radio, and he needed help. He suggested that because of his message he wasn't getting the support he needed to stay on the air. But, if you haven't taught anyone how to prosper, and if they are too broke to support you, it's not difficult to see why you might have to go off the air.

Press On to Your Blessed Future

Let's take a look at what the apostle Paul had to say about obtaining his own success in God.

> *Not as though I had already attained, either were already perfect.*

—Philippians 3:12

Many times unbelievers misunderstand Christianity because they say that we think we're perfect. However, every real Christian knows better. We've all got problems to deal with, and we all have plenty of flaws on which we're working. No one is exempt.

Therefore, don't judge and criticize other people, for everyone is on his or her way to a destiny in Christ. Some of us will have to conquer a drug addiction. Others will need to overcome a sex addiction. Some of us will need to cast off a poverty mentality, and many of us will need to be healed from an abusive childhood. There are even those among us who will have to overcome being neglected and overlooked and made to feel small. Whatever you may be facing right now that you need to overcome, I know this: if God be for you than who can be against you? God has locked arms with you, and He won't let you fail.

I've been in situations in which I've said, *Oh, Lord, how are we going to do that?*

God's response is always reassuring. He says, "Don't worry about it. I did not bring you this far to leave you."

At times you need to reason to yourself by considering that God did not save you in order for you to fail. He didn't bring you out of Egypt in order for you to die in the wilderness. You may not know how He's going to make circumstances and situations work, but He will work them out. You may not know from where the money will come, but make up your mind to believe that it's on the way. You may not know when your breakthrough will take place, but choose to believe that it's on the way.

When You're Tempted to Quit

When you feel like quitting, the Holy Spirit may be saying, "Not today, for your breakthrough is coming tomorrow."

Let's examine the apostle Paul's words:

> *Not as though I had already attained, either were already perfect: but I follow after, if that I may apprehend that for which also I am apprehended of Christ Jesus. Brethren, I count not myself to have apprehended: but this one thing I do, forgetting those things which are*

behind, and reaching forth unto those things which are before, I press toward the mark for the prize of the high calling of God in Christ Jesus.

—Philippians 3:12-14

In other words, the apostle was saying, "Look guys, I haven't arrived either. But this one thing I do—and you, too, must do this one thing. Before you do steps six through nine and fifteen through thirty, you've got to do this one thing. You must choose to keep pressing on, to keep going, to make up your mind and set your course forward—no matter what." He said,

Let us therefore, as many as be perfect, be thus minded: and if in any thing ye be otherwise minded, God shall reveal even this unto you.

—Philippians 3:15

He said, if you're thinking any other way than this, God is going to show you. So don't rebel when He tries to show you that you are thinking incorrectly.

Paul said,

Not that I have now attained [this ideal], or have already been made perfect, but I press on to lay hold of (grasp) and make my own, that for which Christ Jesus (the Messiah) has laid hold of me and made me his own.

I do not consider, brethren, that I have captured and made it my own [yet]; but one thing I do

[it is my one aspiration]: forgetting what lies behind and straining forward to what lies ahead.

I press on toward the goal to win the [supreme and heavenly] prize to which God in Christ Jesus is calling us upward.

—Philippians 3:12-14, (AMP)

Paul is telling us that we've got to be focused on the goal and we've got to stay focused. When you lose focus you lose momentum; you're easily distracted or swayed off-course.

When you navigate a boat while the wind is blowing it makes slowing down very difficult as you move through a channel. If you slow down too much, the wind can blow you completely off course. If you lose your momentum it becomes increasingly difficult to keep the craft in the channel.

Your life is no different. When you are on fire for God you are in church every time the doors are opened. Nevertheless, there are plans, plots and schemes by the devil to rob you and destroy you. When your spirit was full of fire you didn't even notice those plots and schemes because you were moving in the things of God. But when you slowed down—or when you got distracted by the world—you experienced resistance that you wouldn't have noticed had you kept moving at full speed.

Stay Focused

When you slow down you start hearing people say, "Who does she think she is?"

You were moving so slowly that you heard that. You weren't focused. You were just meandering into the church. Instead of coming early, you showed up for praise service twenty minutes late. Because you're moving so slowly and not focused, other people will distract you. They can even cause you to feel bad about what God has ordained for you. So stay focused.

The apostle Paul said he hadn't yet arrived, but he was on his way. What about you? The same passage reads a little differently in The Message. It says:

I'm not saying that I have this all together, that I have it made. But I am well on my way, reaching out for Christ, [or the anointing] who has so wondrously reached out for me. Friends, don't get me wrong: By no means do I count myself an expert in all of this, but I've got my eye on the goal, where God is beckoning us onward—to Jesus. I'm off and running, and I'm not turning back.

So let's keep focused on that goal, those of us who want everything God has for us. If any of you have something else in mind, something less that total commitment, God will clear your blurred vision—you'll see it yet! Now that we're on the right track, let's stay on it. Philippians 3:12-14, (The Message)

This is where I live, because I don't feel that I have it all together. But I'm on my way. There are things that I need to learn, but I'm willing to learn them. There are many things that need changing in my life, but I'm willing to change.

Never lose your focus and never start looking around at all that's going on around you. Don't let circumstances affect and distract you and make you want to quit. Isaiah 43:18-19 says,

Remember ye not the former things, neither consider the things of old. Behold, I will do a new thing.

Divorced people have a problem with this. Statistically, 70 percent of those who get married for a second time end up getting divorced. Often the reason is that they continue to remember the former things — the problems of the previous failed marriage — and they transfer all the hurt, pain and failed expectations from one marriage to another. They set up little barriers to protect themselves from being hurt again, and these barriers block the growth and intimacy needed to create a new marriage.

Thus, they never really let the new person into their lives. They don't really trust that new partner who's done nothing to hurt them and only attempted to love them. The previously hurt partner then places the new partner on the defensive, forcing that one to make a full-time job out of proving his or her love.

From this day on, determine that you will not let your past shape and limit your future.

About eighteen years ago I was an alcoholic. If I let the defeat of that period of my life shape my future, I could never walk in the confidence I need to fulfill God's calling on my life. Every time that

He tried to bless me, I'd probably reject His blessings because I could never feel worthy enough to receive them.

Many of us were raised in churches that taught us that we were little more than filthy rags; we were good for nothing and would never amount to much. You'd pray, "I know I'm unworthy, but I'm beseeching you, Jesus, help me now."

That kind of thinking is unscriptural. The Bible says you are the righteousness of God through Christ Jesus (see 2 Cor. 5:21). Christ is your righteousness, but if you are the salt of the earth, as the Bible says, how then can you be salt and a dirty rag?

God tells us, "Behold, I will do a new thing" (Isa. 43:19). God is doing a new thing in your life. No one even knows you anymore because you've changed. This passage continues:

> *Behold, I will do a new thing; now it shall spring forth; shall ye not know it?*
> —Isaiah 43:19

God promised us that He would make roads in the wilderness and rivers in the desert. Now, who wouldn't want to serve a God like that? People may be concerned that the stock markets are drying up, but they don't know the power of God.

Conclusion

God has promised us that our future in Him is brighter than ever. We can never keep our eyes on the past and let ourselves be weighed down by previous mistakes. Only in God can we find liberty and freedom to embrace a bold, bright future. So set your mind for it. We won't know that this new thing has arrived if we're not looking for it.

Expect things to get better. You're not going down and you're not going under. You're going over. This will be your best year ever, because you are part of a generation that will excel beyond all expectation.

Chapter 8

Reject The Grasshopper Mentality

The Israelites got a preview of their Promised Land during a visit. There, they saw giant grapes and a land flowing with milk and honey — all that God had promised. But they couldn't appreciate the prosperity they saw because they also saw giants who made them feel like grasshoppers. If you are going to cross over into the success and prosperity that God has for you, you must reject their grasshopper mentality.

Do you have a grasshopper mentality? If so, you must get rid of it, for it will hold you back from success. Let's take a look at the pitfalls of this mentality so that we can learn how to avoid it.

God told the Israelites to visit the Promised Land, for He had already given it to them, and it was a part of their covenant. All they needed to do was go down there and take possession of it.

Numbers 13:30-32 says:

> *And Caleb stilled the people before Moses, and*
> *said, Let us go up at once, and possess it; for*
> *we are well able to overcome it.*

But the men that went up with him said, We be not able to go up against the people; for they are stronger than we.

And they brought up an evil report of the land which they had searched unto the children of Israel, saying, The land, through which we have gone to search it, is a land that eateth up the inhabitants thereof.

Caleb told the Israelites that they were not speaking according to God's word. We can learn from Caleb. When the enemy is coming in, when there's discouragement coming your way, then what God tells you to do you must do quickly. If God tells you to give, don't wait three months to obey Him. Go on and do it right away.

The Israelites opposed the wisdom of Caleb's words. That's why you must watch who you have around you. You must be selective about whom you're hanging out with. Sometimes your family will pour discouragement and doubt upon you. Now, you cannot stop loving them, but there are times when you cannot afford to surround yourself with people whose doubts will bring you down.

The Israelites claimed that the land God was bringing them into ate up its inhabitants. But were that true, then the Canaanites wouldn't have been there. Doubt and unbelief always make things appear much worse than they actually are.

In America, the media will announce that we're having a gas shortage. But if that were actually the case, then why do they keep selling it? If there were a genuine shortage, you have to know that efforts would be made to preserve it. In such instances, all that's being preserved is somebody's bottom line.

Every time a storm or hurricane whips through Florida, tearing up property, we generally hear an announcement declaring that our homeowner's insurance premiums will need to be increased because of the disaster. But why do they raise the rates? They've been making billions of dollars off us for years.

The same thing happens with respect to car insurance. When you have a wreck they want to raise your rates. It doesn't matter that you've been driving your car for 15 years and have paid $30,000 over that time to insure your car in the event of a collision. When you actually have a wreck and it costs $3,000 to repair your vehicle, you are notified that your rates are going to increase. But that's why you purchased insurance in the first place — in the event that you had a collision.

These companies raise our rates because they can and because they want to continue making the same profit. It's not that there's a shortage of anything — it's all about profits.

The Bible says that the earth is the Lord's, and the fullness thereof (see Ps. 24:1). The earth is full of everything, which means that God's not bankrupt. Heaven's not bankrupt, either. The earth contains plenty of provision for the six billion people on it. There's enough water, food and natural resources for every person on the earth. The only reason that starvation exists is that some folks are greedy and won't allow others to get anything.

We Were Grasshoppers

Don't buy into the mentality that says we're suffering from shortages. There's no shortage of money. This attitude of lack gives rise to the grasshopper mentality. Let's examine this mentality a little more closely.

And they brought up an evil report of the land which they had searched unto the children of Israel, saying, The land, through which we have gone to search it, is a land that eateth up the inhabitants thereof; and all the people that we saw in it are men of a great stature.

> *And there we saw the giants, the sons of Anak,*
> *which come of the giants: and we were in our*
> *own sight as grasshoppers, and so we were in*
> *their sight.*

—Numbers 13:32-33

This is that grasshopper mentality. In our ministry, we strive to defeat this kind of mentality by being the very best at everything we do. We plan to build the biggest and best, which is God's best for us.

We plan to build the largest sanctuary in the continental United States. Some folks say that we're being arrogant to say such a thing. But someone already has the largest, and if we build ours bigger I guarantee you that someone else will build another one that is bigger still. That's the order of God. One man's obedience to God only cuts the path for somebody else to obey God. We're on television today because somebody went on Christian television before us.

How Do You See Yourself?

The Israelites saw themselves as grasshoppers. The verse says, "And we were in our own sight as grasshoppers, and so we were in their sight."

According to this passage, how you see yourself will determine how others see you. That's why I walk around as if I own everything. If my daddy owns it then I own it, too, because I'm an heir. I have an inheritance in God. The Bible says that I'm a joint heir with Christ Jesus and the throne of God (see Rom. 8:17). I'm not a grasshopper; I'm royalty!

You are God's Unlikely Choice

If you feel that you are too inadequate and simple for God to choose, then you must realize that the criteria He uses to choose you are different from the world's. He chooses the foolish thing, and if you feel foolish then you are first in line. God chooses the unlikely—like you and I—to do awesome things. Look at this:

But God hath chosen the foolish things of the world to confound the wise; and God has chosen the weak things of the world to confound the things which are mighty; and base things of the world, and things which are despised, hath God chosen, yea, and things which are not, to bring to nought things that are. That no flesh should glory in his presence.
—1 Corinthians 1:27-29

The reason that God has given me a vision is not because I'm smart or because I'm such a good businessman, even though God has anointed me to do many things. The reason He gives me success is because He is God—not because I'm me. God will work in and through your life to help you do what He's called you to do, not because you're you but because He is God. When you understand this principle it relieves you of a great deal of stress.

No More Excuses

Each of us has a destiny, and we have no excuse for not fulfilling it. You have a purpose, and if you didn't have a destiny, you wouldn't exist. You have no excuse for failure, for the Bible teaches that failure is something you choose. As long as you have an excuse for your failure then it is an option that you've chosen instead of choosing success.

Look at 2 Corinthians 12:9. God says:

> *And he said unto me, My grace is sufficient for thee: for my strength is made perfect in weakness.*

His grace suggests His ability, anointing and enablement. So you can't say that you're weak and that's why you can't succeed. God says that when you're weak then He is strong in you. He says the weaker you get and the more you turn towards Him in your weakness, the stronger He will be in you. Therefore, your personal sense of weakness is no longer an excuse. As a matter of fact, it's an asset.

We no longer can use our pasts as excuses for our present failures. Look at 2 Corinthians 5:17. It says, "If any man be in Christ, he is a new creature." If you belong to Christ, you no longer have a past. You are a brand-new creature of God.

When I read this scripture, I get so excited. It blesses me to know that now I've got evidence in the Word of God, and Satan cannot use anything in my past against me.

You may have been a lying, whoremongering, dirt dog; a Boone's Farm-drinking, vodka swallowing, joint smoking, crack cocaine-using loser. But when you were born again, God said, "Therefore, if any man..." That includes women, too. We are all new creatures in Christ Jesus.

So, when your old friends and family members tell you what you used to do, you can tell them, "No, no, no—you're talking about a dead man. He's dead and buried. That's the old me."

Now, every now and then that old man will try to creep back in. That's why Paul said that he worked hard to keep his body in subjection (see 1 Cor. 9:27). Even if your old man shows up to dominate your flesh and your thinking, he no longer has any access to you.

Satan will attempt to inject thoughts into your mind, seeking to get your flesh to react to his will. That old flesh nature is what tries to rise up and come back to life. It has a desire that it wants to fulfill but it cannot fulfill its fleshly desire unless you submit to it.

Paul continues:

> *Therefore if any man be in Christ, he is a new creature: old things are passed away; behold all things are become new.*
> —2 Corinthians 5:17

In Christ, I'm a new creature—all things have become new in my life.

God Is Committed to Your Success

God has an awesome commitment to you and me through covenant, and He is faithful to that covenant. Few passages describe the commitment that God has to your success as fully as the story of Sarah and Hagar in the book of Genesis.

You'll recall that Ishmael was not the will of God. He was born outside of God's perfect plan for the nation of Israel. It was never God's will for Abraham to produce an offspring through Hagar, Sarah's maid. But I want you to see the heart of God and the love and kindness of God as reflected in this passage.

> *And Sarah saw the son of Hagar the Egyptian, which she had born unto Abraham, mocking. Wherefore she said unto Abraham, Cast out this bondwoman and her son: for the son of this bondwoman shall not be heir with my son*
>
> ...

—Genesis 21:9-10

You'll remember that Sarah, according to the customs of the day, told Abraham to go to Hagar and produce an heir because she was barren. But later, when God miraculously healed her barrenness and gave her a son, she became upset about Hagar's son.

At first she didn't have the faith to believe that God could heal her barrenness. God had told Abraham that Sarah would produce an heir. But they didn't have much time to wait. Once they became elderly, they began to lose faith. Sarah told Abraham, there's Hagar over there. *Go over there and have sex with her and get a baby, and then God will be pleased.* However, God is not pleased with you and me unless we obey Him, and partial obedience is still disobedience. God told Abraham:

For the son of this bondwoman shall not be heir with my son, even with Isaac. And the thing was very grievous in Abraham's sight because of his son. And God said unto Abraham, Let it not be grievous in thy sight because of the lad, and because of thy bondwoman; in all that Sarah hath said unto thee, hearken unto her voice; for in Isaac shall thy seed be called.

—Genesis 21:10-12

Abraham loved Ishmael, and he was a man of covenant. God is saying, "Yeah, I know that producing Ishmael was wrong, but it was the past." Then, interestingly, God made a promise to Abraham so that the child's future would be established. And also of the son of the bondwoman will I make a nation, because he is thy seed.

—Genesis 21:13

That's the love of God, and that's covenant. God said, "Ishmael wasn't My will, but because of My covenant and because he's your seed, Abraham, I'm going to bless him." Did Ishmael deserve to be blessed? Absolutely not, for his birth wasn't a part of God's design, but God blessed him anyway.

When a young lady has a child out of wedlock it is wrong. But God is still in the business of redemption. Now that the baby is here, it's time to bless the child. The best we can do for that child is to honor it and raise it up to serve the Lord.

God helped Abraham to get beyond his past mistakes. He couldn't go back and change the past. Nevertheless, since Ishmael was in the land, God chose to bless him because of God's gracious covenant.

Too often we refuse to let go of the past instead of allowing the past to die. For generations, a child is ridiculed because of the circumstances of his or her birth. And sadly, the baby is an innocent victim.

That's why I hate to hear parents refer to their children as stepchildren. "This is my son George, and this is my stepson Harry." Either Harry is your son whom you've adopted into your family by covenant or not. What does "step" mean anyway? Does it imply that one child is somehow less than the other? God didn't give Ishmael less than Isaac because God loved him just as Abraham loved him.

The Power of Covenant

Sarah treated her maid Hagar, together with Hagar's son Ishmael, very harshly. Let's look.

> *And Abraham rose up early in the morning, and took bread, and a bottle of water, and gave it unto Hagar, putting it on her shoulder, and the child, and sent her away: and she departed, and wandered in the wilderness of Beer-sheba.*

> *And the water was spent in the bottle, and she
> cast the child under one of the shrubs.*
>
> *And she went, and sat her down over against
> him a good way off.*
>
> —Genesis 21:14-16

This mother was a victim of Abraham and Sarah's lack of faith. And here she is rejected, broken and in great emotional and spiritual pain. She doesn't understand what's gone on. She's probably reasoning, "I haven't done anything but obey my masters. I did as I was instructed, and now I'm thrown out into the desert to die with little more than a bottle of water."

She places her son under a bush and then she moves away from him. Sounds like a lot of families we know. She said,

Let me not see the death of the child. And she sat over against him, and lift up her voice, and wept.

> *And God heard the voice of the lad; and the
> angel of God called to Hagar out of heaven,
> and said unto her, What aileth thee, Hagar?
> Fear* not; for God hath heard the voice of the lad
> where he is.
>
> —Genesis 21:16-17

Interestingly, it doesn't say that God heard Hagar, and she didn't have a covenant. But God said he heard the voice of the boy. How much more will God hear your voice because you have a covenant?

Are you seeing the power of covenant here? This is a child, but he's a child with a covenant. Folks, stop thinking low thoughts about yourselves. Stop putting yourselves down. Again, Romans 8:1 says that there is, therefore, now—right now—no more condemnation, no more judgment against those who are in Christ.

God said,

> *Arise, lift up the lad, and hold him in thine hand; for I will make him a great nation. And God opened her eyes, and she saw a well of water; and she went, and filled the bottle with water, and gave the lad drink.*
>
> —Genesis 21:18-19

Remember, He will make a river in the desert. Isn't that awesome? That's the kind of God we serve. God is so in love with you and me that He won't let the devil have an advantage over you. The only way you lose is when you quit and refuse to hear God. Hagar and Ishmael could have died in the desert had Hagar decided not to hear God and obey.

Walking as a Covenant Child

Every time I think about all of the pain and the injustice suffered by those who have been adopted it grieves my heart. You see, I was adopted, and I'm well aware of how painful the childhood can be of one who has been adopted.

There are parents that will take a child in their home, and because that child did not come out of their loins, they'll buy one child new clothes and give the other child old rags. That's not right.

Those who get married after already having had children are now called blended families. But there is no such thing as a blended family. Either it's a family with a covenant or it's not. A family is one when God puts it together. We've got to love like God loves —unconditionally.

It's not difficult to give that unconditional love when we understand God's unconditional love towards us. He loves you with a love that's so great that your mind could never fully comprehend it. And God accepts you just as you are, so much so that He's made a powerful covenant with you that He will never neglect to honor.

Never again think of yourself as a grasshopper, for you are royalty, a child of the King of kings.

Chapter 9

Know That Timing Is Everything

If you ask, most powerfully successful individuals will tell you that timing is everything. The right timing is a powerful key to unlocking your success. Therefore, let's investigate this amazing key so that you can discover how to open any and all doors in God's perfect time.

A close look at the life of Solomon shows us that he refused to hurry. Solomon, the wisest man who ever lived and probably one of the wealthiest, was not in a hurry about anything. Let's find out why that was so. If you can learn to follow Solomon's lead with respect to timing, you will find that from this day forward you'll be able to live a life of success the way that Jesus did.

This principle of timing can be seen in 1 Kings 6:38:

And in the eleventh year, in the month of Bul, which is the eighth month, was the house finished throughout all the part thereof, and according to all the fashion of it. So was he seven years in building it.

When we read about the "fashion of it," the verse is literally speaking of completing construction on the details of the temple's craftsmanship.

When I saw this I got very excited. Solomon was seven years in the process of building the temple. If you study the Bible about this amazing building project, you'll learn that King David, Solomon's father, left him enough money, building materials and resources so that he could have rushed the project and completed it in far less time. But Solomon chose not to go that route.

And I like the word "fashion," or "detailed," here. Have you ever done detailed work on anything? If so, you know that delicate, finely detailed work cannot be rushed. If your outcome is going to be excellent, you will need to pay painstaking attention to the details. When you do, your results will be excellent.

Many people have asked me when our building project will be completed. They want to know, "Have you finished yet? Have you started building yet? What stage of building are you in?" We started building when we let the words come out of our mouths. Nevertheless, we don't intend to rush this project. We're determined to wait upon God's perfect timing.

Solomon took the time necessary to develop essential relationships with kings, skilled craftsmen and thousands of workers before they ever laid one stone upon another. How often do we want to start a project before we've completed all the necessary preparations? We know that God spoke to us, but we're tempted to rush ahead.

Time Provides the Help You Need

In addition, God rarely calls an individual to accomplish a great task all alone. I'm sure there have been times in which you started something because you knew God had spoken to you, but no one had yet come alongside you to help. You might have been ready, but your help was not yet ready. Perhaps your help needed a little more development time.

Solomon waited until everyone God had called to the project had been assembled together. If you read the accounts of Solomon's life, you'll learn that he met with kings. He met with carpenters who knew wood. He met with craftsmen. He met with all the people necessary for the highly detailed work to be done properly.

In his book, *A Millionaire's Common Sense Approach to Wealth*, Christian author Dexter Yeager discusses the power of learning the right timing. He also addresses waiting, calling it a weapon.

Although they never taught us this in school, understanding timing and learning how to use the weapon of waiting can make you a skilled negotiator.

When I was in business and management, working as a training manager of Magic Market stores, I attended classes on negotiation skills. We learned how to negotiate and reason with many types of people. One aspect of negotiating was learning how to reveal as little information as possible during negotiations. Therefore, it's important not to talk much.

That method actually is consistent with what the Bible says. The Scriptures teach us to be quick to hear and slow to speak. A person with whom you're negotiating really doesn't know where your power points are and where your weaknesses are until you open your mouth.

Often it's the weapon of waiting that keeps you from becoming a part of that person's plan instead of him or her becoming a part of your plan.

Waiting comes into play when you purchase land, as well. Whenever you have an opportunity, I encourage you to buy land. Some wise businessmen and women buy land that they hold on to for ten, fifteen or twenty years. They purchase at a very low price when it's still undeveloped and later they sell it at a significant profit. Waiting is essential, for it is important to hold the land long enough to see the investment grow.

Holding it for that amount of time suggests that you are a person who's not in a hurry. Nevertheless, anything that is truly significant in your life will require time. Anything that's important, anything of any significance at all will take time to develop and time to be perfected.

Every time you get in a hurry, you destroy, by rushing, the very thing you're attempting to create. Too many people get in a hurry and mess up.

Avoiding the Pitfalls of Rushing

Rushing can lead you into many snares, and it can rob you of the success that you've worked so hard to realize. Therefore, you will need to overcome the pitfalls of rushing to experience lasting success. Let's take a look at some pitfalls to which you may be prey when you hurry.

We've all made purchases and later regretted that we didn't take more time. You may have a car right now that you didn't buy. Somebody sold it to you. There is a difference. I once sold cars, so I know.

Let me show you something you probably hadn't thought about. In an average successful car dealership, the salesman may spend a minimum of one to two hours every day perfecting the art of closing a sale.

That means that he's spending from five to ten hours a week learning how to sell you a car. And if you're not prepared to wait during the process of negotiating your sale, you may go in wanting a red car and driving out with a blue one.

Why did you buy that blue car when you wanted a red one? You may not even know why. I remember when I was in car sales, this is what they told us: if an individual came on the lot, he or she was a potential buyer. You may just think you're there to look. However, you don't look for what you don't want to buy. That makes you a potential buyer.

As a salesperson, I've got to learn what it would take to sell you a car on the day that you walk onto the lot. I ask, "What do we have to do, Ms. Jones, to make you happy?"

Some car dealers do crazy things to get people to buy a car. One ploy is called "de-horsing" you. That means the dealer would give you a set of keys and let you take the car home for the weekend without a contract. That puts a lot of pressure on you. When you get that car home around your family and friends, you'll feel embarrassed if you don't buy the car. The dealer puts pressure on you to deal with him in his timing and not your own. You get into a hurry, and before you know it you've spent a lot more than you needed to spend.

A wise man will increase in learning, according to the Word of God. Therefore, let's take a look at some pitfalls of rushing.

Haste Makes Waste

The first pitfall is the fact that when you hurry you increase the mistakes you make. We all know that to be true. Every time you get in a hurry, you mess up. The old adage says, if you don't have enough time to do it right the first time, you will have even less time to do it all over again. So take your time and do it right the first time. Abram and Sarai learned that rushing would cause them to make major mistakes. Let's look.

After these things the word of the Lord came unto Abram in a vision, saying, Fear not, Abram: I am thy shield, and thy exceeding great reward.

And Abram said, Lord God, what wilt thou give me, seeing I go childless, and the steward of my house is this Eliezer of Damascus. And Abram said, Behold, to me thou has given no seed: and, lo, one born in my house is mine heir. And, behold, the word of the Lord came unto him, saying, This shall not be thine heir; but he that shall come forth out of thine own bowels shall be thine heir.

—Genesis 15:1-4.

Here we see that Abram is worried that he will not produce an heir. He tried to come up with a solution that God will accept, since God does not seem to be bringing the promised child into their lives.

God tells him that the heir will come forth from him, but really it means from both him and his wife, Sarai.

In chapter 16 we find that problems arise because they got in a hurry. They couldn't wait until God manifested their answer in His own way. Generally speaking, most of us Christians are as guilty as Abram and Sarai of this same thing. We know what God said; we are certain we've heard Him. There was absolutely nothing wrong with what we heard. Yet, we can't wait for God to do it.

Marriages are particularly susceptible to this pitfall. Two people know that they have found the right one in each other, and the marriage is ordained of God. As a matter of fact, the institution of marriage is a God idea, not a world idea. Therefore, the couple feels there's nothing wrong with rushing into matrimony. But because they enter into marriage too hastily, they end up having to deal with a raft of problems that they might otherwise have avoided.

> *Now Sarai Abram's wife bare him no children: and she had a handmaid, an Egyptian, whose name was Hagar. And Sarai said unto Abram, Behold now, the Lord hath restrained me from bearing: I pray thee, go in unto my maid; it may be that I may obtain children by her.*
>
> —Genesis 16:1-2

Now, is this what God said? No, not at all! But Sarai and Abram yielded to the notion that they could speed up the process a little bit. I don't think that Sarai was sitting down trying to figure out how it was all supposed to come about. Perhaps old Abram was getting a little tired of waiting.

I think old Abe just probably put a little pressure on her until she just finally said, "Look, whatever."

Can you imagine? Sarai is an old lady who never had any children. And, here, old Abe, all he talks about is having an heir. Before long they were helping God.

Enough pressure will cause you to make adjustments in your thinking regarding God's Word, even if you don't agree with the decision you made under pressure. Look at verse 3 and 4:

And Sarai Abram's wife took Hagar her maid the Egyptian, after Abram had dwelt ten years in the land of Canaan, and gave her to her husband Abram to be his wife. And he went in unto Hagar, and she conceived: and when she saw that she had conceived, her mistress was despised in her eyes.

The fact that Hagar despised Sarah really upset Sarah, and when she got upset she blamed Abe. Now, you know there's something wrong with that, right? Why would Sarah get so upset after she has finally conceived if this other arrangement were completely her own idea? In a desperate moment, they rushed the process of God — rushed His perfect timing and created an enormous mess.

We know that every word of God is true. The Bible affirms this truth in Numbers 23:19 when it says, "God is not a man, that he should lie; neither the son of man, that he should repent." If God says He'll do it, He will. If He speaks, He'll bring it to pass.

God would have brought Abram and Sarai's promise to pass, but they got in a hurry. Abram never resisted the idea of going into Hagar. So as a result of his getting in a rush, he went in to Hagar, and they created Ishmael.

Hagar's son was a legal heir, and the Bible says that Hagar was Abram's wife. The only problem was that Ishmael wasn't the heir God promised them.

> *And he went in unto Hagar, and she conceived: and when she saw that she had conceived, her mistress was despised in her eyes. And Sarai said unto Abram, My wrong be upon thee: I have given my maid into thy bosom; and when*

she saw that she had conceived, I was despised in her eyes: The Lord judge between me and thee.

—Genesis 16:4-5

So we see that the man got in a hurry, and as a result they created a problem that exists even today. Ishmael became the Arab nations that have opposed the Jews for thousands of years.

So when you hurry you increase the mistakes you make. And there are mistakes you can make by getting in a hurry that you keep on paying for.

Take Time So You Don't Need to Do It Over

When you hurry, you often have to redo everything you have done. You get in a hurry to get married and you may end up being married more than once. If we had married in God's perfect timing, we would never need to marry again.

On your job, when you rush, you become much less efficient and effective. Before long, you're producing at a poor quality level.

Take Time to Follow Uncommon Achievers

When you slow down a little you are able to follow the example of other uncommon achievers.

There's a myth about high achievers that many of us believe. We see high achievers as being like hummingbirds who are always expending enormous amounts of energy. They have huge bursts of energy and then they just burn out.

This really is a myth. If you watch uncommon achievers you will notice that they are often people who have a great deal of patience and are very observant. It's impossible to be observant and notice details when you're always in a hurry. Those who are in a hurry will see the wide and broad road but they'll miss the narrow road. When you miss details, you miss excellence.

You need to slow down so that you can be sure you're headed in the right direction. Make sure that whatever you're doing, you're doing it in the best way possible.

Take Time for Wise Counsel

Another reason to slow down and get God's timing is so that you will have enough time to seek out wise counsel. Don't get too busy to listen, to hear and to be counseled. The Bible says that wisdom is found in a multitude of counselors.

I have sons in the ministry whom I don't see. They might think that they don't need counsel now. But obtaining counsel as we grow will keep us from failing later. If we don't take time to get counsel now, we might get into our tomorrow and find we're deficient.

I have a busy schedule and I travel all around the country and internationally. But I still take time to go sit under my spiritual father to get his counsel. I make the time to do it. You will always make time for what you consider important.

That doesn't mean that you need to have a counseling session with that person. It only means that you need to get to that leader's church and hear the Word and receive it. That's when you're going to get the very best counsel if you have ears to hear and eyes to see. The Spirit of God will be there to minister to your exact needs, regardless of what the sermon subject may be.

If you don't take the time necessary to get wise counsel, then somewhere down the road you will need that Word, but it won't be in your spirit. Slowing down provides time to receive worthy counsel.

One Hurried Moment Can Create a Month of Chaos

One hurried moment can cost you a month of chaos. As a matter of fact, one moment of rushing, or hurrying, can produce a whole lifetime of chaos.

There are people who are in trouble today that they can't get out of because they got into too much of a hurry. They didn't read a contract all the way through before they signed on the dotted line. All they would have had to do was read the contract. If they didn't understand it, they should have taken the time to contact an attorney.

Being in too much of a hurry can result in financial chaos in your life, your business or your home.

Remember this: Satan pushes you, but the Holy Spirit leads you. You can learn to live a directed life and not a driven one. The sons of God are led, not pushed.

I don't care how great a deal you think it is, don't hurry to make the purchase. There's always another deal.

A car dealer will try to convince you that you need to make a decision immediately. That's what he's trained to do. Ask yourself why you need it so fast. Is the dealership going out of business? If so, perhaps you shouldn't buy it there anyway.

Perhaps the seller is telling you that this car is a forty year-old antique. You have to buy it right now. But if it's been around for forty years, where's it going? One more day won't matter much. Tell the dealer that you'll be back tomorrow, and then go home and pray about it. Purchases always look different after you've had a chance to sleep on them. Never purchase anything on emotion.

I love to shop, but there's a big difference between shopping and buying. Shopping is going in the store, looking at an item you want and comparing prices. Afterwards, go to three or four more places so that you'll know you're getting the best deal.

Everything is on sale. The price starts out inflated and is then dropped down to a more reasonable level. But that doesn't necessarily mean that you're getting a deal. When you're in a hurry, you won't know if you're getting the best price.

You see a blouse with a regular price of $125.00, and it's marked down to $89.99. You assume that it's a good deal. But if you shopped around a little more, you would find the same blouse in another store for $69.

Never Let People Hurry You On Important Projects

When you let another person's panic and pressure rush you on a project at work, it will only hurt you in the long run. Never let people hurry you or rush you on important projects. If it's important then take your time. If it's really important, you're better off if you take all the time you need.

Never buy things in a hurry just because someone is pushing you. Don't make an important decision when you feel pressured. You'll be stuck with the outcome because you came under the control of someone's pressure.

Eliminate Buyer's Remorse

Have you ever gone somewhere and made a purchase that you regretted later? By refusing to hurry, you'll never experience buyer's remorse.

Perhaps you spend money you have earmarked for something else because you get talked into making a foolish purchase. Before you even get home, you feel overcome with remorse. You say, *Oh, man, I blew it!*

You may well have clothes sitting in your closet that you've never worn. They've been hanging here for months and they still have the tags on them. Do you know what that represents? It was the seed for your harvest that was misallocated, misappropriated. See, when you come up short on your harvest, it may be due to not sowing the right seed somewhere.

Once, around Christmas time, I almost bought a dual recording VCR. My son Bryan was with me, and thank God for the wisdom in a child. I forgot how much it was, which was about $900. I was getting very emotional about the purchase — very excited, talking about how I could tape tapes and record one tape off the other.

Bryan asked me one question after the salesman went in the back to get one for me to buy. He said, "When are you going to use it? What are you going to use it for? Dad, you have a VCR now, and when have you ever recorded anything?"

All my VCRs flash 12. I don' t even know how to program them. I ask my son to make recordings for me, and here I am thinking of buying two. I would have had some serious buyer's remorse.

What about exercise equipment? You have all of that equipment that you haven't used in years and you haven't lost an ounce of weight. Your treadmill has been sitting in your bedroom catching dust and providing a nice place to hang your clothes. You've got a $300 clothes rack and you've got buyer's remorse.

Pray about all of your major purchases. Deborah and I have a rule concerning major purchases. I don't ever buy anything major without discussing it with her. The Bible says you should delight yourself in the Lord, and He will give you the desires of your heart. Let God bless you and quit trying to bless yourself. You'll only end up in trouble.

With any major purchase, especially if you're married, make sure that husband and wife both agree on the purchase, or it's not the right time. Now, that's hard for some of you, but if you're both born again and you don't agree then your prayers are hindered, according to Peter. You're a house divided against itself.

Look back at the biggest mistake you have made in your life, and you'll probably find that you had been in a hurry.

Don't Hurry Into Marriage

Allowing another individual to hurry you into marriage can create a lifetime of heartache. If something on the inside of you is telling you that this is not the time, then listen to your own heart.

Are you pregnant out of wedlock, and you want to give the baby a name? Don't marry a fool who will give both you and your child a lifetime of heartache. You should have considered that before you had sex. But since you didn't, don't compound the problem by getting into a hasty marriage that could bring disaster upon you. You could still be dealing with the problem twenty years later, after your youth, your opportunities and a lifetime of unhappiness have passed.

If you need to be rushed, then you're not ready. And your knower (your heart) may well be trying to tell you that you're not ready. If you overlook the guidance of peace, you're going to have a problem that you'll have to deal with for the rest of your life.

Don't tell yourself that you'll just get a divorce if things don't work out. Divorce doesn't erase. Statistically, 70 percent of the people that have been married for the second time get divorced.

When I counsel those who are getting remarried I ask them what makes them think they can do it right this time. Marriage is not a 50/50 proposition. It's two whole, mature individuals who should be prepared to be assets to one another — 100 percent assets. Marriage can never be one needy person trying to find some other needy person.

Take time to get to know the person you want to marry. See him or her in all kinds of situations. Find out how she reacts when she's mad. Find out how responsible he is with his money.

Is he going to lose his temper and start slapping you? You ought to know that before you get into a bad marriage. Will she lie to you and flirt with your friends? Find out whom you are marrying.

Don't wait until after you're married to discover some surprises. You shouldn't have any surprises.

Investigate Before You Invest

I always said it like this: investigate before you invest. Before you invest your life or your life's savings, investigate, because your losses can be very heavy if you don't. You can experience losses that you may never recover. Some people end up so damaged and bruised that they can never again trust another person. Don't become the walking wounded. Take the time you need to make wise choices.

Conclusion

Take the time you need to do it right, and you'll never have to go back and heal broken hearts and wounded spirits. You'll never have to drive home feeling the pangs of buyer's guilt and remorse. You'll never sign contracts that will lock you into a lifetime of loss, nor will you rush through a project at work and be blamed for errors and mistakes. One of the greatest keys to lifelong, enduring success is taking the time you need. So never forget — timing is everything!

Chapter 10

Don't Sacrifice Your Future for Immediate Pleasures

Instant gratification is wanting what you want—and wanting it now! But getting all that you want when you want it can cause you to sacrifice your future and throw away greater success. Therefore, never sacrifice your future success for the sake of immediate pleasures. Arm yourself with a willingness to defer gratification, and you will soon discover this to be one of the most powerful weapons in your arsenal of success.

Let me explain. Solomon produced a dream at his highest possible level of excellence. When you want to produce at the highest possible level of your own excellence you will need to defer gratification, which sometimes means that you will need to pay a present price for future rewards.

Making Wiser Decisions

Are you in an apartment? Why not get out of that apartment and into a starter house? Do you know what a starter house is?

It's a place that needs a lot of work, but it's cheap, and you can own it. It's far better to live in your own house that you've got to fix up then to pay for somebody's yacht in that apartment that's already painted and carpeted.

Now, I'm not telling you to live in the ghetto. I'm just telling you there's a better way to manage your money by making wise decisions.

Before God renewed my mind, I would have struggled with this concept. When Deborah and I were first married, a lady tried to talk us into buying a house. It would have cost us about $300 per month back then to own this house, and we were paying about $155 to rent.

I reacted as if the lady was out of her mind. We went to look at the property, and I felt that it didn't have much to offer. But I didn't know any better. I would have owned that piece of property and could have later resold it for a much larger place. Instead, I wasted a lot of money on renting a nicer looking apartment and had nothing to show for it but payment receipts. When you buy a house you're sinking money into something that you own.

Back then I preferred renting an apartment in a more upscale area to owning property in a less impressive location. Today, I'd rather own a house anywhere than rent in the best apartments in town.

When you defer gratification, or you wait to live in the kind of place you really want, it will pay off for you over the long run. Even if the house has small bedrooms and a postage stamp yard, you're going to build equity—equity that you can use to get into what you really want. That small home you own becomes an asset.

Therefore, make your purchases by being led by the Holy Ghost about what to buy and when.

Deborah and I bought the house we now live in two years ago. Recently, the realtor told us that our property is worth $80,000 more than what it was valued when we purchased it two years ago. That's not counting all the equity that's accumulated since we bought it. Do you know what that means? It means that we have more equity in our current house than our previous house cost. And we've only lived there two years. So start where you are and build. That's what it means to defer gratification.

You say, "Well, Pastor, I've got to have a down payment to buy a house." That's true, but there are lots of ways to make that down payment. You might have a V.A. loan available to you that will let you get into a house with no down payment. You may be able to work out a deal with an anxious seller. No matter what, determine to start saving today. Don't make major purchases; put the money in the bank instead. Get rid of cable and use the monthly fee to start a savings program for your house. You've got some money coming in from somewhere, so develop a plan and get started.

Stop sacrificing your future for the sake of immediate pleasures and wants. A friend and I were discussing this matter. It's interesting how you can really miss God by getting into debt—by creating debt while trying to enjoy instant pleasures. Debt isn't necessarily a sin, but you have to know when to incur a debt and when doing so is unwise. Avoid incurring debt on depreciating items, such as cars, clothing, food and entertainment.

Never borrow in your present at the expense of your future. Only use debt today as an investment into your future. For example, in buying a house Deborah and I didn't have funds to cover the cost of our house in savings. But we did have enough money to make a down payment to get into the house. And as a result of that initial investment, we earned over $80,000 in equity in the house in two years.

There were plenty of other things we could have done with the money we used as a down payment on the house. But anything else would have meant using it for immediate pleasures.

For Americans, our greatest investment is going to be our house and land. You need to invest in that before you invest in the stock market or anything else. It will usually yield your highest return.

Land is one of the best investments you can make, because it's not going anywhere. No one's making anymore of it. Go find some land in a rural area for a few thousand dollars and hang on to it.

I remember when my uncle bought some land in the country for $2,500. He has made money off of that land by growing trees on it. He cut down the trees and sold them to pay off the property. He and his wife know that they will always have that land to live on some day.

Resisting Instant Rewards in Communication

The way in which you conduct yourself in business also provides opportunities for you to defer gratification. If you need to be liked, to be seen as a big spender or to be seen as important in other peoples' eyes, you may end up saying more than you need to in business negotiations. But if you learn to say very little, instead of being seen as wise, you will walk away being truly wise.

Let's look at this. King Solomon refused to say too much in his conversations with others. Are you in trouble today because you tend to say too much?

I've learned the art of negotiation. One day, I was speaking to a man who owned a business on a piece of property that our ministry was seeking to purchase. We believers have an advantage because we have the Holy Ghost helping us. As I was speaking to the man about purchasing the property, he went into a typical seller's mode, seeking to justify the high price he wanted for the building.

The more he talked, the less I said. I explained to him that we didn't need his business, just the land for additional parking.

He talked more and more about the business on the property. As I listened, I determined a fair price for the property based upon our use and not upon the business that had been located at the site. We needed to negotiate a fair asking price for the real value of the property.

When I determined a very fair asking price, I stopped negotiating. I stayed right there, regardless of what he said or did. I had the Holy Ghost helping me to come up with the right offer.

The more the man spoke, the more he revealed what he wanted to get for the property, which was far more than we were willing to pay. As he spoke on, he revealed a great deal of information that we were able to use to help us negotiate a far better price—with the help of the Holy Spirit.

He told me to set a price, to make him an offer, but then he revealed the price he wanted through his many words. Because his price was far too high, we refused to get emotional about the sale. We pulled back and just waited. When the Holy Ghost is working with you, He provides the wisdom you need to negotiate good contracts.

Having the control to wait out a negotiating process is a way to get the best possible deal.

Always negotiate from a position of strength; this means that you should never be in a hurry to negotiate a fast deal based upon emotion.

In this particular process of negotiations, we had to show the seller that we were willing to not get the property. It would just be more convenient for us if we had it for parking.

So don't be hasty in your words or with your conversation. Don't get in a hurry. Always be quick to hear and slow to speak. Proverbs 29:20 says it this way:

Seest thou a man that is hasty in his words?
There is more hope of a fool than of him.

Negotiations with Believers

When you are negotiating with Christians your negotiations should be different. When you're dealing with a brother or a sister in the Lord, just pray and do whatever the Holy Ghost tells you to do. Say what He tells you to say. He will fill your mouth with words of wisdom if you ask Him.

Wise and Unwise Decision Making

Unlike financing a home, buying a car can cost you a great deal more money over time. That's because an automobile doesn't appreciate as does a house. For example, if you purchase a $25,000 car at 10 percent interest, that vehicle will end up costing you $37,500 over five years.

That's a major investment, which you should get into very prayerfully. You would be paying $625 a month for five years—money that could be producing a harvest for you. If you rush and make this kind of decision out of emotion, you can delay a harvest of blessings that God wants to send your way, all because you didn't defer gratification.

You may shop around and get better monthly payments if you purchase the car. You may even decide to lease the car for the greatly reduced rate of $380 a month for three or four years. But at the end of those three years, you're in even worse shape because you own nothing.

If you purchase the car, your $25,000 car that you paid $37,500 over a five-year period of time will be worth about $9,000, if it's still in excellent condition. Major purchases are important decisions. Therefore, don't sacrifice your future for immediate, emotional gratification or pleasure.

Conclusion

My prayer for you is that God would give you a spirit to discern the areas of your life in which your decision-making is based upon emotion and not sound wisdom from the Word of God. I pray that you would learn to defer gratification; doing so is the mark of a wise and prosperous man or woman.

Chapter 11

Go the Distance

The demands of today's world often can feel like a pressure cooker, and as you increase in success, your levels of stress may increase, too. Therefore, in order to go the distance, investing in seasons of personal restoration will be one of the wisest decisions you can make.

You need to take some time during your daily routine for personal restoration. It won't take all day, and you don't have to go on a vacation to accomplish what I'm telling you. You just need to take some time. Sometimes all it takes is the time required to transition from work to home. You simply need to get somewhere and get quiet for a few minutes during your day.

You may feel as if you're resting when you sit down and watch television, but then you watch things that upset you. Television can actually cause you to end up being more upset and more stressed out. You are much better off just taking thirty minutes to chill out.

Jesus took time away from the crowds to recuperate and restore Himself. In my own life I've discovered that this principle of wisdom is vital to my ongoing success. Not all of us function exactly the same way. Some of us need a lot of little breaks. Others require an occasional longer break. You will need to find out what works best for you. Whether you need long breaks or short ones, it is still essential that you restore yourself.

That's one of the reasons that I go and sit under the teaching of my spiritual father from time to time. We all need to be fed. If I'm constantly pouring out all the time, I also need to receive. Preachers who never sit under someone who has authority over them and can speak or make deposits into their lives will find themselves preaching or ministering out of an empty spirit. When you minister out of an empty spirit it can lead to depression.

You'll notice great spiritual leaders who start off strong and do very well, but they never go to a quiet place where they can be restored. Sooner or later they start to look beaten down and tired. They have neglected this principle of success and are reaping serious consequences.

Prepare for the Long Haul

Don't let yourself get so drained that you end up becoming ineffective and unproductive. Balance activities that drain your spirit. Remember, you're in this for the long haul. Determine to go the distance and be as refreshed at the end as at the beginning.

If you recall the story of Moses, this mighty leader had placed himself in a position to become burned out. He was counseling with people all day long and completely spending his strength working through their various problems and crises.

Moses' father-in-law, Jethro, who had been a spiritual leader for years, gave him some wise advice that allowed him to go the distance. Jethro came to Moses and told him to bring in seventy additional leaders whom he could train and to whom he could impart his own spirit. These leaders where then able to help Moses in his work with the people.

Some of my own church members have gotten upset with me because they wanted me to be continually available for counseling. I decided that I would counsel with people on Thursdays. I then informed those seeking counseling that they would need to make an appointment on Thursdays. I also decided to limit my counseling sessions to thirty minutes.

In addition, I also hired two individuals to assist with counseling. If a person has an emergency or can't wait until Thursday, that person can meet with another counselor. My busy schedule required me to limit my availability for counseling sessions.

If someone in my congregation still insists on speaking to me outside of my scheduled counseling times, I encourage him or her to write a letter, which I promise to read. Jethro told Moses that he was seeing people from the morning to the evening and was draining his own spirit. Moses was literally wearing himself out. No doubt the first few people received some pretty good counsel, but after his spirit started to get drained his effectiveness probably started to diminish somewhat.

That's why I've reduced the number of people I counsel. When you are counseling people continually, all of their burdens, needs, rebellion, anger and other baggage begin to drain your spirit. You end up with people on the brain and people in your spirit. You need to back away at times to pray. I go and get on my boat and go out on the water, or I get on my bike and just ride. That's when I can pray, get some quiet time with God and feel restored. Then I'm ready to go back into the battle.

I preach almost every day. I preach on Tuesday, Wednesday, Friday and three times on Sundays. I have one day off—Monday. In between all of that, as CEO, I manage the business side of the church.

Because I do have a busy schedule and because I have a lot of things that God has called me to do, I take a lot of breaks. These breaks are required to rebuild and restore my spirit.

Sometimes I'll leave one service and just go outside to walk around in order to refocus for the next service. The reason for this is that the people who come to second service are not the same people who attended the first service. I've got to clear my spirit of the first service so that I can effectively minister in the second service. That's why even if the message is the same it always comes out differently. I may use the same scriptures, but the message will be presented to the needs of the group.

Come Apart For Rest

Jesus Christ Himself actually made time in His ministry for times of restoration and refreshing. In doing so, He laid down the pattern for other ministers to follow. Let's take a look:

And when his disciples heard of it, they came and took up his corpse, and laid it in a tomb. And the apostles gathered themselves together unto Jesus, and told him all things, both what they had done, and what they had taught. And he said unto them, Come ye yourselves apart into a desert place, and rest a while: for there were many coming and going, and they had no leisure so much as to eat.

—Mark 6:29-31

Jesus and His disciples were so busy meeting people's needs that they didn't even have time to eat. Jesus told them, "You all need to go take a break." What that break was designed to do was to provide time for restoration for a rebuilding so they could be fresh.

Staying fresh for ministry is essential. Sometimes I'll bring two suits to church. I started doing this because we didn't have air conditioning in our former building. Now I sometimes bring a change of suits just because it feels like a fresh start.

Nevertheless, you still need to take that time away. Deborah will go home and just go off by herself.

It doesn't need to be longer than thirty minutes or an hour. It doesn't take all day. You just need a time of rest. There's something that needs to be restored in you. If you've been depositing into others, then you need to be refilled.

Conclusion

You're in the race to win. Your success will be largely determined by how you've finished. Starting out well and burning out halfway will cause you to fail and fall.

It doesn't matter from where you started. You may have started defeated, busted and broke. But if you finish by meeting your goals, your life will be a success and you will be a champion in Christ.

So run to finish; stay in the race no matter what. Keep steady and pace yourself with times of refreshing and restoration, and success will be yours in everything you set out to do!

The Vision of the Truth Domes

For the past eight years, it has been the vision of Pastor Powe to build the Truth Dome. The Truth Dome is a 15,000 seat auditorium that is dedicated solely for use by the Body of Christ.

In September of 1999, God multiplied Pastor Powe's vision by three. With the help of 250,000 Truth Partners, Pastor Powe now plans to build three Truth Domes. One will be in Tampa, the second in the Southwest and the third on the West Coast.

The Truth Domes are convention centers to be used by the Body of Christ. They will be built BY Christians, FOR Christians with the sole intent of reaping the end-time harvest of souls into the Body of Christ.

For more information on becoming a Truth Partner with Greg Powe Ministries, please call us at (800) 601-1414.

Other Books By
Pastor Greg Powe

The Blessing

Having The Peace of God

BIG Vision BIG Provision

The Purpose of The Promise

The ABC's of Faith

Spiritual Warfare

Faith Purpose and True Prosperity

Believers or Make-Believers

3 Signs of True Prosperity

Why We Need The Word

The Demands of Stewardship

For more information on products offered by Pastor Greg Powe
or to order products, please contact us at:

1-888-41-TRUTH

www.revealingtruth.org